THE GOLD

1975

text: David Sandison, Michael Heatley, Lorna Milne, Ian Welch

design: Yael Hodder

Welcome to *The Golden Years* and the comings, goings, faces, places and events which shaped 1975.

The comings included the arrival on the world stage of Pol Pot and his Khmer Rouge communist forces, and any temptation Westeners may have had to shrug him off as just another tinpot revolutionary in some unimportant far-away country soon evaporated as we began to hear of the horrors his regime was inflicting on the people of Cambodia. Also new to the international spotlight was Margaret Thatcher, voted the new leader of Britain's Conservative Party in succession to a deflated Edward Heath. Little did anyone know what that item of news would mean!

We all knew what the fall of Saigon meant - that the 30 years of war the people of North and South Vietnam had endured, along with the families of French and US soldiers who'd been killed or injured during their countries' interventions in that war - was finally over. Unhappily, what would prove to be another long and bloody conflict would have its first violent beginnings in Beirut.

Much of Europe suffered the chaos of terrorist action, with London, Vienna and Amsterdam all targeted. The Soviet authorities made physicist and human rights campaigner Andrei Sakharov a target

5

when he was awarded the Nobel Peace Prize, and the all-conquering West Indies cricket team achieved their target of winning the first-ever World Cup in England.

Martina Navratilova decided to seek asylum in the US, New Zealand athlete John Walker decided that a man could run a mile in less than three minute 50 seconds (and did), the editors of *Time* and *Newsweek* decided to herald the arrival of a new rock star, Bruce Springsteen, on their covers in the same week, and Jack Nicholson decided that the system should be bucked in *One Flew Over The Cuckoo's Nest*.

It's all in these pages, and a lot more besides.

JANUARY 5

Coggan Is New Archbishop Of Canterbury

The Reverend Donald Coggan, who previously taught theology at Wycliffe College in Toronto and at the London School of Divinity before becoming Bishop of Bradford, today became the new Archbishop of Canterbury, taking over from Michael Ramsey, who retired at the end of last year.

During his five years in office, Archbishop Coggan would become best known for supporting the ordination of women and heralding a break with Anglican tradition which was to split the Church for many years to come. He also advocated closer links between Protestants and Catholics via shared communion among the clergy.

JANUARY 2

The Sweeney Bursts Into British Homes

The first British police drama series to be filmed on the streets of London, *The Sweeney* hit UK television screens for the first time tonight, destined to be a huge immediate and long-term hit. Starring John Thaw and Dennis Waterman, *The Sweeney* took its name from the cockney rhyming slang for Flying Squad - Sweeney Todd - and portrayed the police of that Scotland Yard department in a way which was far removed from the cosy image created for the London bobby' by series like *Dixon Of Dock Green* in the 1950s.

Its high-speed car chases, use of firearms and often racy dialogue courted controversy, but *The Sweeney* - which regularly attracted almost 9 million viewers - ran for three years and would set the trend for many future TV crimefighter series. Waterman would go on to pop stardom and another long-running series, *Minder,* while Thaw would play a rather gentler cop, the studious *Inspector Morse,* in the late 1980s.

JANUARY 2

Giant UK Oil Company Collapses

The British Government and the Bank of England were today forced to step in to bail out Burmah Oil, Britain's second largest oil company, after it announced huge losses. The rescue bid was made in an effort to boost London's flagging Share Index, which dropped to a 20-year low as Burmah Oil's collapse wiped more than £1,000 million off the value of other shares.

A combination of unexpected losses in tanker operations and the company's over-ambitious acquisitions programme was thought to have caused the financial shortfall, which left the oil giant unable to repay huge debts.

JANUARY 4

Pol Pot Puts Phnom Penh Under Pressure

THE CAMBODIAN CAPITAL, Phnom Penh, was reported to be under siege today, suffering constant heavy artillery and rocket attacks by Communist Khmer Rouge guerrillas in what observers believed was an all-out bid by Khmer Rouge leader, Pol Pot to bring his five-year campaign to a victorious conclusion.

At this time in Cambodia's complicated and confusing history, very little was known about Pol Pot, who would later conduct a three-year purge in which millions of Cambodians died – the notorious 'Killing Fields'. Aged 47 and a fanatical hard-line communist, he was known to have the backing of Cambodia's former ruler, Prince Sihanouk, then living in exile in Beijing. Pol Pot's forces were armed by the Chinese, who were determined to help him oust the pro-Western regime of Marshal Lon Nol.

While the US Embassy, and American companies heavily committed to Cambodia were preparing plans to evacuate personnel in the increasingly likely event of the city falling to the Khmer Rouge rebels, commanders of Cambodian-based US forces developed contingency plans to airlift supplies in an attempt to repel them.

Despite this show of strength, Pol Pot's forces had been encouraged to believe they could win the war by the recent US decision to cut $200 million from its military aid bill to Cambodia.

UK TOP 10 SINGLES

1: Streets Of London
- Ralph McTell
2: Down Down
- Status Quo
3: Lonely This Christmas
- Mud
4: The Bump
- Kenny
5: Never Can Say Goodbye
- Gloria Gaynor
6: Ms Grace
- The Tymes
7: Get Dancing
- Disco Tex & The Sex-O-Lettes
8: I Can Help
- Billy Swan
9: Wombling Merry Christmas
- The Wombles
10: My Boy
- Elvis Presley

5

ARRIVALS

Born this month:
22: Balthazar Getty, US actor

DEPARTURES

Died this month:
8: Richard Tucker, operatic tenor, aged 60
16: Paul Beaver, US pop synthesizer pioneer *(Beaver & Krause)*
24: Larry Fine, US film comedy actor *(The Three Stooges)*
28: Antonin Novotny, Czech President 1953-68, aged 70

JANUARY 9
Inflation Overtakes UK Economy

In London today, the Labour government announced pay increases of up to 74 per cent for 14,000 public sector workers in a month when wage inflation rose to 28.5 per cent. Even its most loyal supporters were hard-pressed to deny Opposition leader Edward Heath's accusation that inflation had overtaken the economy and dramatic remedies were needed.

Newly-published figures showed that over 25 per cent of pay rises were now breaking the government's Social Contract, an agreement with major trade unions designed to curb pay rises.

In February, miners would accept a pay rise of 35 per cent, while their employers, The Coal Board, announced that coal and other solid fuel prices would have to go up by 30 per cent as a consequence.

As fuel costs soared out of control, the price of a gallon of petrol rose from 42p to 72p, with VAT (Value Added Tax) increases levied by Chancellor Healey last November only worsening the situation.

JANUARY 1
Arise, Sir Charlie!

One of Britain's most famous sons, the legendary comedian, writer, film director and producer Charlie Chaplin (pictured), won the nation's highest award of recognition today when he received a knighthood in the traditional New Year's Honours List.

Sir Charles, as he was to become, was raised in appalling poverty in London, but escaped to join the Fred Karno Company in 1906, when he was only 17. Discovered by pioneer US film producer Mack Sennett, he began making short comedy films and developed the tramp character which would make his fortune and timeless reputation.

Via international hits like *The Kid, City Lights, The Gold Rush, Modern Times* and *The Great Dictator,* Chaplin became an immensely rich and internationally popular star. In the 1950s he found himself the subject of investigation by the notorious Senator Joe McCarthy's Un-American Activities Committee and left the US to settle in Switzerland. He did not return to the US until 1971, when he was presented with a Special Oscar to honour his contribution to the cinema.

JANUARY 1

Mitchell, Haldeman And Ehrlichman Jailed For Watergate Cover-Up

WITH DISGRACED former President Richard Nixon safe from prosecution, thanks to the complete pardon awarded him by President Gerald Ford last August, other senior US Government figures and Nixon aides were not so fortunate. As court hearings into the Watergate conspir-acy continued to claim heads, three of the biggest catches found themselves adjudged guilty in Washington today.

Former Attorney-General John Mitchell and ex-confidants Bob Haldeman (Nixon's Chief of Staff) and John Ehrlichman (his former Domestic Adviser) were convicted of conspiring to obstruct justice during Congressional investigations into the illegal wire-tapping of the Democratic Party's 1972 presidential election campaign headquarters in the Watergate office and hotel complex.

When sentenced on February 21, the three would receive jail sentences of between two and a half and eight years for their part in the cover-up, which involved paying hush money to the men involved in the burglary. Mitchell's Assistant Attorney-General, Robert C Mardian, was also sentenced to a prison term from ten months to three years.

JANUARY 16

Freedom At Last For Angola

After nearly 60 years of exercising direct rule, Portugal - whose associations with the West African nation of Angola dated back to 16th Century slave-trade days - today announced its decision to give the colony its independence.

The independence agreement was due to come into force on November 11, with a transitional government holding power in the intervening months, pending a democratic election.

As Angola had been racked by a civil war for the past 13 years, the prospects for peace did not appear great. The three factions waging that war - the MPLA, FNLA and UNITA - seemed unlikely to agree on forming a coalition government.

FEB

FEBRUARY 11

Margaret Thatcher Becomes New Tory Leader

A MIGHTY BLOW FOR WOMEN in politics was struck in London today when 49-year-old Margaret Thatcher won the Conservative Party's internal election to become Britain's first leader of a major political party. She beat four men, including the incumbent, former Prime Minister Edward Heath, in the process.

Mrs Thatcher, married to wealthy businessman Denis Thatcher and mother of son and daughter twins, was originally from Grantham, Lincolnshire, and had studied chemistry and law before entering politics full-time.

She won the first ballot against Edward Heath to score a decisive 130-119 victory. In the final vote she beat her main rival, senior politician Willie Whitelaw, by 146 to 79, with fellow candidates Geoffrey Howe, James Prior and John Peyton trailing the field with fewer than 20 votes each.

Relations between Mrs Thatcher and her predecessor, who resigned disconsolately on February 4 after the first ballot, were - and would continue to be - decidedly cool, and there would be no place on her future teams for him. But although the defeated Whitelaw couldn't disguise his disappointment when, with tears in his eyes, he promised 'We unite behind her', he would prove a man of his word, becoming a valued adviser and friend to the new leader.

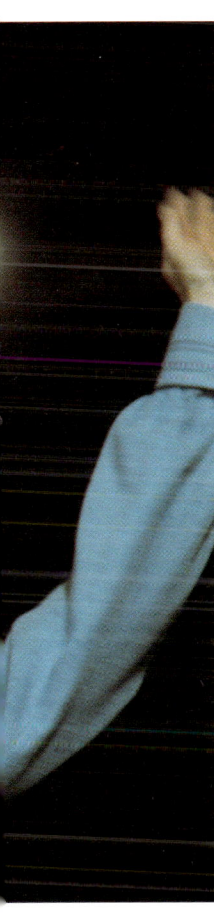

FEBRUARY 14

Comedy World Mourns 'Plum' Wodehouse

Awarded a knighthood only last month in the New Year's Honours, Pelham Grenville (PG) Wodehouse, the comic writer best known for his creation of Bertie Wooster and his indispensable valet Jeeves, died today at the age of 94.

Known to his friends as 'Plum', Wodehouse also found success in musical comedy, theatre and films. Upon leaving school he embarked on a career in banking which was quickly abandoned in favour of writing – a career which began with short stories in *Punch* and the *Strand Magazine* and eventually resulted in 120 books. It was *The Man With Two Left Feet*, first published in 1917, that introduced a delighted public to Jeeves and Wooster.

Living in the French resort of Le Touquet in 1940, Wodehouse was imprisoned by the Nazis and, though released, was prohibited from leaving France. He advisedly agreed to broadcast to the Allies, causing a row in England, although what he said could hardly be termed propaganda. Nevertheless, after the war he decided to settle in the US, where his parodies of the English aristocracy never failed to give pleasure.

FEBRUARY 12

Robot Relations For Ross

The Stepford Wives, a major film adaptation of William Goldman's best-selling novel, starring Katharine Ross of *The Graduate* and *Butch Cassidy* fame, was the big film premiére in Hollywood tonight.

It told the story of a wife new to a commuter suburb outside New York who gradually discovers that all her female neighbours have, at their husbands' behest, been replaced by computerized models!

In a decade when women were still fighting to take their place alongside men in society, *The Stepford Wives* was a chilling reminder that, for some men, the 'ideal' woman is not born, but made.

Not that the new Conservative Party leader would agree...

UK TOP 10 SINGLES

1: **January**
- Pilot

2: **Goodbye My Love**
- The Glitter Band

3: **Sugar Candy Kisses**
- Mac & Katie Kissoon

4: **Please Mr Postman**
- The Carpenters

5: **The Bump**
- Kenny

6: **Morning Side Of The Mountain**
- Donny & Marie Osmond

7. **Angie Baby**
- Helen Reddy

8: **Ms Grace**
- The Tymes

9: **Never Can Say Goodbye**
- Gloria Gaynor

10: **Make Me Smile (Come Up And See Me)**
- Steve Harley & Cockney Rebel

ARRIVALS

Born this month:
22: Drew Barrymore, US film actress (*ET*, *The Amy Fisher Story*, *Little Girl Lost*, etc)

DEPARTURES

Died this month:
4: Louis Jordan, US musician, singer, bandleader *(see main story)*
14: Sir Julian Sorell Huxley, British scientist and philosopher, aged 87; Sir PG Wodehouse, British-born US comic author *(see main story)*
24: Nikolai Bulganin, Soviet ex-premier, aged 80
28: Sir Neville Cardus, English cricket and music writer, aged 85

FEBRUARY 26
IRA Suspect Kills London Policeman

A chilling reminder of the IRA's deadly intentions in mainland Britain came today when an off-duty London policeman, 21-year-old Stephen Tibble, was shot dead at point-blank range after he'd gone to the aid of detectives chasing an IRA suspect.

During a round-up of known IRA sympathizers following PC Tibble's murder, Scotland Yard believed it had uncovered evidence that the IRA was about to launch yet another series of bombings on the capital, when a bomb factory was discovered in West London.

A national operation began to track down the killer of the young policeman who, like the vast majority of his colleagues on and off duty, was unarmed.

FEBRUARY 4
Jordan, King Of Jumpin' Jive, Dies

Louis Jordan, the American singer, bandleader and alto sax player, died in Los Angeles today, aged 66. Known as 'King of the Jukeboxes' after his version of Johnny Mercer's *GI Jive* became one of the most-played records in US Army bases in 1944, his music had a direct effect on the birth of rock 'n' roll, via the producer Milt Gabler, who reputedly based his productions of Bill Haley's hits on his work with Jordan.

The music of Jordan and his band, The Tympany Five, would inspire UK singer Joe Jackson to record an album of covers, *Jumpin' Jive*, in 1981, while a stage musical written around his music, *Five Guys Named Moe* - the title of his 1942 hit - would become a long-running London West End success in the 1990s.

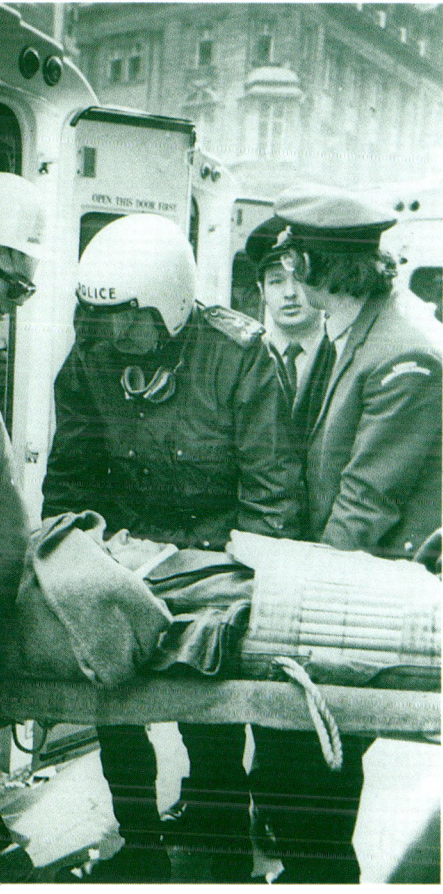

FEBRUARY 28

35 Die In Worst Ever London Tube Train Disaster

ENGLAND'S CAPITAL WAS STUNNED today when 35 people - driver Leslie Newson and 34 of his passengers - were killed as a crowded London Underground tube train ploughed into a dead-end tunnel at Moorgate Station in the City of London during this morning's rush-hour.

Travellers who witnessed the tragedy from a platform reported that the train shot through the station at what seemed like double the normal speed, rather than stopping as scheduled.

The 8.37 from Drayton Park ploughed through sand and buffers at the end of the 80-yard tunnel with such force that the first coach was telescoped into just two feet. Fire, police and ambulance rescue teams called to the scene to free those trapped in the wreckage had to work in diabolical conditions. Stifling heat and dust combined to make their task almost impossible, though the need for speed was crucial as they fought to release the hundreds of injured inside the coaches.

A full investigation started immediately into what was, and remains, London Underground's worst disaster.

MARCH 1

Lovely Livvy Wins Through

Having made her name in Britain with a string of hits, Australian singer Olivia Newton-John conquered America today when she won two trophies in the prestigious Grammy Awards presentations. Her *I Honestly Love You* was voted Record of the Year, with the 27-year-old also presented with the award for Best Female Pop Performance. Newton-John, who was once engaged to The Shadows' guitarist Bruce Welch, went on to find favour with the massive US country music audience before winning lasting fame as the winsome Sandy opposite John Travolta in the movie musical *Grease*. Her fellow Grammy winners tonight in New York included ex-Beatle Paul McCartney, whose *Band On The Run* album also picked up two awards.

MARCH 9

Castro Conspiracy Revealed

A CIA plot to assassinate Fidel Castro, the Cuban President, in the early 1960s was revealed by two US Government officials, Adam Walinsky and Peter Edelman, today.

The two, who worked in the office of Attorney-General Robert Kennedy at the time, insisted that Kennedy discovered a CIA plan to use Mafia hit-men to carry out the killing, and that he was instrumental in stopping the murder attempt.

Documentary evidence would emerge in May to prove that the plot had existed. In June, Sam Giancana - a Chicago Mafia boss implicated in the CIA plot - was shot dead outside his Illinois home.

MARCH 7

Manhunt Launched As Black Panther Kills

British police launched a major manhunt today after the body of the young heiress, Lesley Whittle, who had been kidnapped 52 days earlier by a man calling himself the Black Panther, was discovered in a Staffordshire country park.

Lesley was found at the bottom of a 60ft drain, apparently strangled, only yards from the place where her brother had, under police supervision, arranged with the kidnapper to hand over a £50,000 ransom. The Black Panther, however, never appeared to collect the money. Forensic evidence proved that Lesley had, in fact, died before the planned exchange.

On December 15, a 39-year-old joiner from Bradford, Yorkshire - Donald Nielson - would be arrested and charged with Lesley Whittle's murder. In July 1976 he would be given five life sentences for murder.

MARCH 25

Saudi Arabia's King Faisal Murdered By Nephew

THE ARAB WORLD TODAY mourned King Faisal of Saudi Arabia, victim of a brutal shooting by his 31-year-old nephew, Prince Museid, during a ceremony at the Royal Palace in Riyadh. The King had been a powerful influence in the Middle East and there were real fears that the death of one of the more moderate monarchs of the Islamic world would destabilize the region.

Faisal had succeeded to the throne in 1964 when he deposed his brother, Saud, and began to pursue a policy of using Saudi Arabia's vast oil revenue to transform and modernize his nation.

Succeeded, in his turn, by his younger brother, Crown Prince Khalid, King Faisal was killed while taking part in an official traditional reception for his subjects on the Prophet's birthday. His assassin, who was known to be mentally unstable, would be beheaded on June 18, in keeping with Saudi and Islamic law.

UK TOP 10 SINGLES

1: If
- Telly Savalas
2: Only You Can
- Fox
3: Bye Bye Baby
- The Bay City Rollers
4: Make Me Smile (Come Up And See Me)
- Steve Harley & Cockney Rebel
5: The Secrets That You Keep
- Mud
6: My Eyes Adored You
- Frankie Valli
7: Pick Up The Pieces
- The Average White Band
8: There's A Whole Lotta Lovin
- Guys & Dolls
9: Please Mr Postman
- The Carpenters
10: What Am I Gonna Do With You
- Barry White

13

DEPARTURES

Died this month:

8: George Stevens, US Academy Award-winning film director (*Gunga Din, A Place In The Sun, Shane, Giant, The Diary Of Anne Frank,* etc), aged 71

14: Susan Hayward, US Academy Award-winning actress (*I Want To Live, With A Song In My Heart, I'll Cry Tomorrow,* etc), aged 56

15: Aristotle Onassis, Greek tycoon, aged 69 (see main story)

16: Aaron 'T-Bone' Walker, US blues guitarist, aged 64

28: Sir Arthur Bliss, British composer, Master of the Queen's Music, aged 83

MARCH 29

Vietcong Capture Key South Vietnamese Cities

SOUTH VIETNAM was in chaos today as Da Nang, its second largest city and one of its most important military strongholds, was overrun by North Vietnamese forces - only three days after the communists captured the ancient imperial capital, Hue, 50 miles away.

With Da Nang, the Vietcong also captured a complex of land, sea and air bases full of US-supplied equipment and stores, inflicting a tremendous blow to the Saigon government's hopes of halting the North Vietnamese advance. Elements of South Vietnam's 1st and 2nd Divisions were reported fleeing from the area, and a number of people were known to have died when they tried to escape by hanging from the undercarriages of aircraft.

The Vietcong victory appeared to have been gained easily as military and civilian officials abandoned their posts, and demoralized South Vietnamese troops began looting whole areas of the city before running away. It could only be a matter of time before the inevitable happened, and the North Vietnamese Army reached Saigon.

MARCH 16

Supermac's Record Haul

England football star Malcolm Macdonald wrote his name large in the record books today when he became the first player ever to score five goals in an international at London's Wembley Stadium.

Cyprus were not, admittedly, in the class of West Germany, England's opponents in their previous game (in which Macdonald had also scored), but his single-handed haul without reply against the weakest team in the group suggested the national team, under new manager Don Revie, might yet qualify for the quarter-finals of the European Championships – a hope that would later be extinguished by Czechoslovakia.

MARCH 31

Iraq Pounds Kurdish Rebels

Kurdish rebel bases in the mountains of northern Iraq were attacked by six divisions of Iraqi Army troops today in the newest battle of what had already been a 20-year war between Kurds, trying to establish the independent homeland promised them at the end of World War I, and successive governments in both Iraq and Iran.

The Iraqi attack on rebels led by Mustafa al-Barzani was made possible by Iraq's recently signed peace treaty with the Shah of Iran. This freed the kind of military force the regime in Baghdad believed was necessary to wipe out al-Barzani's rebels altogether.

MARCH 15

Aristotle Onassis Dies

The international world of business, and the gossip column writers of the day, lost a genuine character today with the death of the Greek shipping magnate, Aristotle Onassis. Aged 69, he left his heirs holdings worth $500 million.

Onassis's early business acquisitions meant that he controlled the Allied oil tanker fleet when World War II broke out, and he would gain substantial profits during the course of the war. In 1950, during the Suez Crisis, he found the golden lining in others' clouds when cargo ships and tankers were forced to take the longer, and more profitable, route around the Cape.

Most famous for his affair with opera-singer Maria Callas and his marriage to President John F Kennedy's widow, Jackie, in 1968, Onassis was never far from the centre of the jet-set scene. He had been ill for some while, affected by the debilitating disease *myasthenia gravis*, and was said never to have recovered from the death of his son Alexander in a plane crash two years previously.

15

NICHOLSON TRIUMPHS AS CUCKOO'S NEST FLIES HIGH IN OSCARS

Nominated for a Best Actor Oscar for the third year in succession, Jack Nicholson must have wondered if his performance in Milos Forman's *One Flew Over The Cuckoo's Nest* would break the duck of 1973's *The Last Detail* and last year's *Chinatown* - both of which popular opinion had said had been good enough to deserve little gold statuettes.

He needn't have worried. Although he faced strong competition from Walter Matthau's superb old vaudevillian in *The Sunshine Boys,* Al Pacino's jumpy gay bank robber in *Dog Day Afternoon,* Maximilian Schel's impressive Nazi war criminal in *The Man In The Glass Booth* and James Whitmore's quirky *Give 'Em Hell, Harry,* Nicholson would be part of the flood of awards which made *Cuckoo's Nest* the hit movie of 1975.

Voted Best Picture, with Milos Forman winning the Director Oscar, the film also helped win Louise Fletcher her Best Actress award and gave Lawrence Hauben and Bo Goldman an Oscar for the screenplay they'd adapted from Ken Kesey's novel.

Competition for this year's Academy Awards was pretty tight. Nominated with *Cuckoo's Nest* were Stanley Kubrick's *Barry Lyndon,* Robert Altman's *Nashville,* Sidney Lumet's *Dog Day Afternoon,* and the year's runaway box-office smash, Steven Spielberg's *Jaws.*

Oddly, Spielberg was not nominated as Best Director and *Jaws* failed to win nominations for any of its excellent cast. The Hollywood *wunderkind* had to be content with the millions the film made worldwide, which he'd use to create his production empire, and congratulate his sound team for their Oscar, composer John Williams for his award-winning score, and Verna Fields, for her editing trophy.

Although his *Sunshine Boys* co-star had lost out to Nicholson in the Best Actor category, the eighty-something George Burns won a Supporting Actor award for his performance (beating *Cuckoo's Nest* actor Brad Dourif, *Dog Day Afternoon's* Chris Sarandon, *Shampoo's* Jack Warden and *The Day Of The Locust's* Burgess Meredith in the process).

Louise Fletcher had beaten Ann-Margret (*Tommy*), Isabelle Adjani (*The Story Of Adele H*), 1973 winner Glenda Jackson (*Hedda*) and Carol Kane (*Hester Street*), while Lee Grant's Supporting Actress award for *Shampoo* was at the expense of Ronee Blakley and Lily Tomlin (*Nashville*), Sylvia Miles (*Farewell, My Lovely*) and Brenda Vaccaro (the only decent thing in the awful *Jacqueline Susann's Once Is Not Enough*).

Stanley Kubrick's *Barry Lyndon* won four Oscars - for John Alcott's cinematography, Leonard Rosenman's score, art direction and costume design.

The Keith Carradine song *I'm Easy* put Robert Altman's *Nashville* in the winners enclosure, while Frank Pierson's screenplay ensured *Dog Day Afternoon* didn't go home empty-handed.

As usual, a disaster movie - *Hindenburg* - carried off the sound effects and visual effects Oscars.

So, pretty well everybody got something. Including - at last - Jack Nicholson.

No Oscar for *Jaws*

APRIL

APRIL 12

France Mourns Showbiz Legend Josephine

One of France's most well-known and popular entertainers, the American-born singer and dancer Josephine Baker (pictured), died today at the age of 68, her death marked by the kind of public grief usually associated with the passing of a major political figure.

Born in St Louis, Miss Baker gained her initial fame for her risqué act at Paris' Folies Bergére in the 1920s. She emigrated to France when racial prejudice impeded her career in the US. Her exceptional ability as a dancer and singer was matched only by her sometimes bizarre stage presentations.

Taking French citizenship in 1937, she became active in the French Resistance during World War II. In 1963 she returned to the US briefly, to join Martin Luther King's civil rights march on Washington DC. She left a family of no fewer than 12 adopted children, whom she called her 'Rainbow Tribe'.

APRIL 17

Cambodia Falls To Khmer Rouge Communists

COMMUNIST KHMER ROUGE forces took control of Cambodia's capital, Phnom Penh, today after three and a half months of siege and five years of civil war. Within an hour of defending government forces being ordered to stop firing, black-uniformed Khmer Rouge rebels controlled a city they had shelled and bombed into near ruin and total submission.

It was not clear whether or not the surrender was followed by a blood bath, but a radio broadcast from the Khmer Rouge suggested that they would take revenge. 'We enter as conquerors', listeners were told. 'We are not here to talk about peace with the traitors of the Phnom Penh clique'.

Who would actually head the new Cambodian Government remained unclear. Exiled for five years in Beijing, former Prime Minister Prince Norodom Sihanouk was reported as designating the task to Khieu Samphan, his deputy. He would exercise power with the other Khmer Rouge leaders.

Supreme among those leaders was the mysterious Pol Pot. It was he who controlled the guerrilla army and their arms. It was he who had plotted and won the five-year war. It was widely believed that a man who had killed more than a quarter of a million of his own people to secure that victory was not likely to hand control to a Prime Minister in exile.

APRIL 13

Conflict Erupts In Lebanon

In Beirut today, right-wing Christian alangists shot at a bus containing 27 Palestinians, starting a wave of sectarian violence which brought normal life in the city to a halt and gradually escalated into a 15-year bloody civil war.

Lebanon - which contained almost equal numbers of Christians and Muslims - had always been deeply divided and the reluctance of President Franjieh to call in the army to quell this disturbance was due to his fear that it would split into factions taking different sides in the dispute.

UK TOP 10 SINGLES

1: Bye Bye Baby
- The Bay City Rollers
2: Fox On The Run
- Sweet
3: Swing Your Daddy
- Jim Gilstrap
4: Love Me Love My Dog
- Peter Shelley
5: Funky Gibbon/Sick Man Blues
- The Goodies
6: There's A Whole Lotta Lovin'
- Guys & Dolls
7: Girls
- Moments And Whatnauts
8: Fancy Pants
- Kenny
9: I Can Do It
- The Rubettes
10: Honey
- Bobby Goldsboro

APRIL 3

No-Show Fischer Hands Chess Crown To Karpov

Russia's Anatoly Karpov became the youngest ever world chess champion at the tender age of 23 today, without having to lift a pawn in anger. He won the title by default when the reigning champion, American Bobby Fischer, missed the deadline for the match which was to have taken place in the Philippine capital of Manila.

Fischer's absence was a protest against the dismissal of his demand that Karpov must win by at least two points to take the title.

Karpov was to hold the world title for a full ten years, before finally being toppled by Azerbaijan's Garry Kasparov.

ARRIVALS

Born this month:
9: Robbie Fowler, England Under-21 international football player
13: Bruce Dyer, England Under-21 international football player

DEPARTURES

Died this month:
5: Chiang Kai-Shek, Chinese statesman, former President of Nationalist China and of Taiwan *(see main story)*
12: Josephine Baker, US-born French entertainer *(see main story)*
14: Fredric March (Frederick McIntyre Bickel), US Academy Award-winning actor *(Dr Jekyll and Mr Hyde, Les Misérables, The Barretts of Wimpole Street, The Best Years Of Our Lives, Inherit The Wind,* etc), aged 77
23: Pete Ham, UK pop musician, songwriter

APRIL 30

US Embassy Abandoned As Ho Chi Minh's Army Takes Saigon

THE WAR IN VIETNAM ENDED today when North Vietnamese forces flooded into Saigon to accept the unconditional surrender of President Thieu's South Vietnam government and army. Their victory ended 21 years of bloody civil war and 15 years of often controversial US involvement in what had always been described as an unwinnable conflict.

Saigon finally fell with little bloodshed and the two nations, created by treaty in 1954 after North Vietnamese forces defeated occupying French troops, were reunited as the Socialist Republic of Vietnam.

The US Embassy – symbol of fading hope for South Vietnamese fearful of the communist invaders – was besieged by people desperately hoping for a way out of the city. Inevitably, most were left behind. However, American nationals, 'friendly' foreigners and favoured high-ranking Vietnamese were airlifted to safety (pictured) aboard US warships waiting in the South China Sea.

After the last US soldiers were rescued from the Embassy roof by helicopter, the building was sacked by the mob, angry at what they considered their betrayal by the US. Saigon was quickly renamed Ho Chi Minh City by the new communist authorities, so honouring the North Vietnamese national leader who had inspired and led their long struggle.

While the people of South Vietnam adjusted to a new way of life under a regime determined to create a utopian socialist state, the citizens of the US began to try coping with the harsh reality that the world's most sophisticated military machine had been defeated by an enemy often armed with little more than faith and courage.

APRIL 9

Wilson Sacks Anti-EEC Heffer

British Prime Minister Harold Wilson today sacked his Industry Minister, Eric Heffer, to signal the severity of the split in his cabinet over British membership of the Common Market. While Mr Wilson was known to have suspended the principle of collective cabinet responsibility until a national referendum decided whether Britain remained a member of the EEC or not, Mr Heffer's increasingly vocal and public anti-Europe statements made his dismissal inevitable.

Known to favour continued British membership, the Prime Minister's position was further complicated on April 26 when the membership of his Labour Party voted two to one to quit the EEC, only two days after official government figures showed that the number of people jobless in Britain had passed the million mark.

APRIL 5

Chiang Kai-Shek Dies, Still In Exile

The exiled former President of China, General Chiang Kai-Shek, died today at the age of 87 in Taipei, capital of Formosa, the island fortress state which he built after being defeated by the Communist forces of Mao Tse-tung in 1949.

After helping to create a Republican army in China in the 1920s, Chiang became President of China in 1928, remaining in power for eight years until a kidnap attempt ended his presidency. Disputes between his Republicans, the emerging communists and the surviving warlords of old China continued, culminating in his defeat in the Chinese Civil War of 1945-9.

Chiang Kai-shek and his Nationalists fled to the island of Formosa (later to be called Taiwan) where they created a dynamic manufacturing-based economy. With US support, Chiang's Nationalist China was the only recognized Chinese nation at the US until 1971, when Mao's mainland regime took over. Chiang's death would allow the United States to finally concede that Beijing had the only legitimate government of China.

MAY

MAY 10
Boston Bussing Row

In a move that was intended to improve race relations in the city of Boston, Federal District Court Judge Arthur Garrity today ordered the Boston School Department to achieve a more even racial mix by busing 21,000 children out of their residential areas to other schools.

Strong resistance, by both black and white parents, to the temporary busing order already in existence cast doubt on the long-term success of this policy, especially when Boston's Education Department chief John McDonough announced his committee's decision to appeal to the Supreme Court.

MAY 6
Hungarian Cardinal Dies In Exile

Cardinal Jozef Mindszenty, the former Archbishop and Primate of Hungary who spent 15 years in the safe asylum of the US Embassy in Budapest following the failure of the 1956 Hungarian Revolution, died today in Vienna, the city which became his home in exile when the Soviets agreed to let him leave Hungary three years ago. He was 83-years-old.

A lifelong opponent of Communism, the Cardinal was first arrested in 1948, and tortured and imprisoned for high treason. Released by the more liberal government during the 1956 reforms which sparked the Red Army invasion of Hungary, he fled to the US Embassy as Russian tanks overran Budapest.

Cardinal Mindszenty's continued opposition to the Vatican's attempts to achieve better relationships with Eastern Bloc regimes had led to Pope Paul dismissing him as Hungarian Primate last year.

MAY 6
TV By Royal Appointment

Edward VII, a new £2 million costume drama funded by Independent Television, with Timothy West playing the title role, Robert Hardy his father, Prince Albert, and Annette Crosbie his mother, Queen Victoria, shot to the top of the UK TV ratings today.

Viewing figures of 8.8 million were achieved by a series for which the current Queen's approval was sought, and secured, to film sequences in a number of royal residences, including Windsor Castle, Sandringham and Osborne House on the Isle of Wight.

MAY 21

Tight Security As Baader-Meinhof Trial Opens

THE TRIAL OF MEMBERS of the West German terrorist Baader-Meinhof group began in Stuttgart today amid unprecedented tight security. But it had to be suspended immediately when gang-members rejected state-appointed lawyers, complaining that they had violated client confidentiality.

Charges against the gang stemmed from activities dating back to the late 1960s when the group – also known as the Red Army Faction – broke away from other radical student movements of the time and began an urban guerrilla war which resulted in six killings, a number of bank raids, the bombings of US military establishments and 50 attempted murders.

Despite the fact that several leading members were behind bars and several had committed suicide, followers of the Baader-Meinhof gang would continue its murderous activities into the late 1970s when, in September 1978, it would claim responsibility for the death of a West German policeman.

Gunmen storm West German Embassy in Stockholm under siege by Baader-Meinhof terrorists

UK TOP 10 SINGLES

1: Oh Boy
- Mud
2: Loving You
- Minnie Riperton
3: Stand By Your Man
- Tammy Wynette
4: Hurt So Good
- Susan Cadogan
5: Let Me Try Again
- Tammy Jones
6: Honey
- Bobby Goldsboro
7: I Wanna Dance Wit'Choo
- Disco Tex & The Sex-O-Lettes
8: The Way We Were/Try To Remember (Medley)
- Gladys Knight & The Pips
9: Sing Baby Sing
- The Stylistics
10: Only Yesterday
- The Carpenters

DEPARTURES

Died this month:
3: Mary Ure, British stage and film actress *(Look Back In Anger, Sons and Lovers, Where Eagles Dare,* etc), aged 42
6: Cardinal Jozef Mindszenty, Hungarian Primate, aged 83 *(see main story)*
13: Bob Wills, US western swing pioneer, bandleader, songwriter *(see Came & Went pages)*
15: Richard Conte (Nicholas Conte), Italian-American film and TV actor *(The Godfather, The Purple Heart, A Walk In The Sun,* etc)
28: Ezzard Charles, American heavyweight boxer (world champion 1949-51), aged 54

MAY 27
Thirty-Two Die In Yorkshire Coach Crash

A PARTY OF BRITISH women pensioners enjoying a day out in the Yorkshire Dales became another horrifying road-safety statistic today when their coach crashed to the bottom of a ravine known locally as Devil's Bridge. Thirty-two of the women, all from Thornaby in Teesside, died in what was Britain's worst ever road crash.

Emergency service rescuers had to cut 43 of the 45 passengers free from the wreckage of the coach, which had fallen 16 feet and landed on its roof after breaking through a stone wall. The driver, whose wife was also on the coach, later died, but survived long enough to tell of the brake and gear failure which caused the catastrophe.

The site was notorious as an accident black spot, being at the bottom of a mile-long stretch of road with a one-in-six gradient.

MAY 16
Japanese Woman Conquers Everest

A 35-year-old Japanese climber, Junko Tabei, became the first woman to conquer Mount Everest today, reaching the 29,028 ft peak with the aid of only one Sherpa guide.

She achieved her objective at 12.30 pm, after a five-hour climb from the 25,000-ft camp occupied by the 16-strong all-female all-Japanese team which formed the successful expedition.

In the 22 years since Everest was first conquered by New Zealander Sir Edmund Hillary, 35 men had made the climb.

MAY 21

Sculptress Dies In Studio Fire

Dame Barbara Hepworth, the sculptress considered to be one of the most important figures in contemporary British art, died in a fire which swept through her home in St Ives, Cornwall, today. Emergency services called to the house where she had her studio were unable to reach her through the flames.

Born in 1903, Dame Barbara studied initially at the Royal College of Art with fellow Yorkshireman Henry Moore. Her striking and sometimes controversial creations graced such locations as the UN building in New York - where her *Single Form* acted as a memorial to her friend, Dag Hammarskjöld - and the Royal Festival Hall in London.

Married twice, first to fellow sculptor John Skeaping and later to the painter Ben Nicholson, Dame Barbara died alone in her Cornish home.

MAY 17

Jagged Glass Grounds Jagger

Just two weeks before his band, The Rolling Stones, was due to embark on a lengthy US concert tour, lead singer Mick Jagger was rushed to hospital today after accidentally putting his right hand through a plate-glass window at Gosman's Restaurant at Montauk, Long Island.

Though the wound required 20 stitches, no lasting damage was sustained and the Stones rolled on as scheduled – to the relief of their record company, the tour's promoters and hundreds of thousands of fans.

MAY 3

West Ham Turn Tables On Moore

England's 1966 World Cup-winning soccer captain, Bobby Moore, was, for once, on the losing side at Wembley today as his former West Ham team-mates beat his current club, the Second Division's Fulham, 2-0 in the FA Cup Final.

Moore, who'd moved across the capital in March 1974, was accompanied by another former national captain, Alan Mullery, but their combined experience could not prevent two goals from Alan Taylor taking the Cup to East – not West – London.

Fulham would have belated revenge in 1995, when they'd beat West Ham 2-1. Sadly, it would be a triumph Moore could not share - he would tragically die of cancer in February 1993.

25

Indira Gandhi Convicted Of Election Fraud

JUNE 12

NOT FOR THE FIRST TIME in her political career nor for the last - the Indian Prime Minister, Mrs Indira Gandhi, became the centre of controversy today when she was found guilty of corruption during her election to the Lok Sabha, the Indian parliament, in 1971. Convicted of using government resources and officials in her campaign, Mrs Gandhi was barred from public office for six years by Justice Jag Lal Sinha in the Allahabad High Court.

The 57-year-old Congress Party leader immediately began what would eventually be a successful appeal against both the verdict and her sentence. Two weeks later, while that appeal was pending, 676 of Mrs Gandhi's chief opponents were arrested in pre-dawn raids and charged under the Maintenance of Internal Security Act.

In July, she would act again, banning most of India's political organizations to give herself almost dictatorial powers. Mrs Gandhi would remain in power until 1977 when she lost her seat in a general election, then return to office in 1980. In 1984, she was assassinated by a Sikh member of her bodyguard.

JUNE 5
Suez Canal Reopens

After eight long years, during which time no traffic passed through it, the Suez Canal was again opened to shipping today. Thousands of Egyptians cheered President Sadat at the opening ceremony in Port Said and ships' sirens gave long blasts not heard since the waterway was closed during the 1967 Six-Day War.

The reopening of this major maritime route was seen as a gesture of peace by Anwar Sadat, but he had nevertheless made it clear that he was seeking a lasting settlement over the Sinai Peninsula, annexed by Israel in the war. It would not be until the early 1980s that Israeli troops withdrew completely from the disputed territory.

JUNE 3
Pelé Hits The Big Apple

Edson Arantes do Nascimento, better known as Pelé and arguably the greatest football player of all time, came out of retirement today when he signed a multi-million dollar contract with New York Cosmos of the North American Soccer League (NASL).

Pelé's record after making his début for the Brazilian club, Santos, in 1956 at the age of 15 was matchless, and included three World Cup campaigns and over 1,000 goals.

Though his unique skills had undoubtedly faded, Pelé's presence helped establish soccer as a competitive sport in the US and, despite the demise of the NASL, the country would become well enough considered in the global game to host the 1994 World Cup.

Pelé would play for Cosmos for two and a half years alongside former West German captain Franz Beckenbauer before retiring permanently in 1977.

JUNE 7
Belgians Reject French Mirage And Buy American

European unity was put at risk today when the Belgian Government announced its decision to opt for the American *F-16* jet fighter over the French-built *Mirage F-1*, rejecting French President Valéry Giscard d'Estaing's recent statements that he expected Belgium to support European industry by buying French.

Instead, the Belgian Government decided to buy 102 of the General Dynamics Company's fighters, as had Norway, the Netherlands and Denmark. General Dynamics softened the blow by agreeing that some of their fighters' engines and electronics would be bought from European companies.

UK TOP 10 SINGLES

1: **Whispering Grass**
- Windsor Davies & Don Estelle
2: **Three Steps To Heaven**
- Showaddywaddy
3: **I'm Not In Love**
- 10cc
4: **The Proud One**
- The Osmonds
5: **Stand By Your Man**
- Tammy Wynette
6: **Sing Baby Sing**
- The Stylistics
7: **The Hustle**
- Van McCoy
8: **The Way We Were/Try To Remember (Medley)**
- Gladys Knight & The Pips
9: **Listen To What The Man Said**
- Wings
10: **Send In The Clowns**
- Judy Collins

DEPARTURES

Died this month:
2: Sato Eisaku, former Prime Minister of Japan, aged 74
4: Evelyn Brent, American silent screen actress, aged 76
28: Rod Serling, US TV playwright *(Twilight Zone, Night Gallery)* and film screenwriter *(Assault On A Queen, Planet Of The Apes,* etc)
29: Tim Buckley, US singer, songwriter

US Beaches Empty As Jaws-Mania Strikes

Six weeks after its release, the film *Jaws* appeared to have succeeded in emptying America's beaches and filling its picture-palaces: one person in eight was already said to have seen it!

Co-producer Richard Zanuck described the first half of the film - when a resort mayor refuses to make a killer-shark's presence public for fear of losing money - as 'a Watergate-style cover-up'.

The second part, he concluded, was 'not about analysing problems, it's about annihilating them'.

Starring Roy Scheider, Robert Shaw and Richard Dreyfuss, *Jaws* was directed by Steven Spielberg, and would prove only his first big-screen blockbuster. He would, of course, go on to mastermind *Close Encounters Of The Third Kind* two years later, *en route* to Hollywood superstardom.

JUNE 21

'Windies' Win First Cricket World Cup

A capacity crowd at Lord's, the London ground which is the spiritual and administrative home of world cricket and headquarters of the Marylebone Cricket Club, saw the West Indies take the game's first World Cup today, thanks to a captain's innings of 102 from Clive Lloyd and excellent fielding by the whole team. The eventual margin of victory over Australia was 17 runs after a 60-over, one-day match.

The inaugural tournament proved an unqualified success, with seven national teams doing battle, including a representative East African side. The semi-finals saw the West Indies easily defeat New Zealand, with Australia knocking out the home team. Australia made a valiant attempt to match the West Indies' 291 in the final, but five run-outs – three by all-rounder Viv Richards – assured the 'Windies' their victory.

JUNE 6

UK Says Yes To Europe – Again!

DESPITE STRONG FEELINGS in Parliament that the idea of a referendum was distinctly un-British, ordinary men and women were given the chance to decide on the UK's future in the European Economic Community today. Results of the referendum showed a resounding vote in favour of Britain staying in what is popularly known as the Common Market – a view supported strongly by the Conservative Party, whose then-leader Edward Heath had taken the country in.

Early fears that interested voters would stay away proved unfounded as almost 26 million voters turned out: results showed that 67.2 per cent were in favour of remaining in the Common Market, and 32.8 per cent against.

The strongest party opposition to the EEC came from a left-wing Labour group, and only two out of 68 counties – the Western Isles and Shetland – voted as a whole to abandon Europe.

ASHE HUMBLES JIMBO IN WIMBLEDON CLASSIC

Wimbledon's legendary Centre Court witnessed one of the most popular victories of the 1970s on July 5 when Arthur Ashe, one of the most elegant, thoughtful and clever players of the modern age, systematically took apart the brash, punchy and more dynamic game of Jimmy Connors, the defending champion.

It was a brilliant display by the 31-year-old Virginian, the first black male to win a Grand Slam tournament - the 1970 Australian Open in 1970 - and a man who'd had the respect in which his fellow-pros held him confirmed in 1974 when they voted him first president of their official body, the Association of Tennis Professionals' Tour.

There was, it must be said, a fair degree of support for Ashe simply because he was facing 'Jimbo' Connors a young man who hadn't yet won the affection of a Wimbledon crowd which still thought he was just a little too brash and flash.

The contrast between Connors' power game and the fluid top-spin ground strokes delivered with unerring accuracy by the former US Army officer could not have been greater. Nor could their between-games behaviour: while Connors fiddled and fretted as he tried to think his way out of the beating he was getting, Arthur Ashe sat, for the most part, in silent communion with himself, eyes closed, his body completely relaxed.

Having taken the first two sets with Connors only able to win a single game in each, Ashe met the 'don't-get-mad-get-even' 22-year-old who'd not only beaten Ken Rosewall in straight sets to become 1974 Wimbledon champion, but had also won the US and Australian Opens. Connors took the third set 7-5.

It only took one break of serve for Arthur Ashe to become the Wimbledon Men's champion for 1975, but he got it to win the fourth set 6-4, as the capacity crowd went wild.

A distinguished ambassador for his sport, Ashe would be forced to retire in 1980 after suffering the first of two heart attacks in 1979. Tragically, a blood transfusion he was given during a second heart operation contained the HIV virus, and Arthur Ashe would die of AIDS-related pneumonia in 1993.

He remained a dignified man to the end, using his fame and popularity to found an AIDS research trust and fight for an unhysterical attitude to the disease just as ably as he had once fought for racial equality and civil rights in the US and South Africa.

LAUDA TAKES WORLD CHAMPIONSHIP TO REVIVE FERRARI'S FORTUNES

It's doubtful whether Niki Lauda, the Austrian Formula One race ace, would have been happier to win his first World Championship in more dramatic fashion than he did this year. He was, after all, one of the more thorough and unspectacular drivers of the time, albeit a consistently victorious one.

But the simple fact was, as he climbed behind the wheel of his Ferrari at the start of the Italian Grand Prix in October, the 26-year-old knew he only had to finish in the points to become champion and give Ferrari their first Constructors' title since 1964.

Lauda's stiffest competition at Monza came, with poetic harmony, from his Ferrari team-mate, Clay Regazzoni. Both managed to escape from the chaos of a chicane pileup just after the start, which eliminated five cars - but not that of Emerson Fittipaldi, the man closest to Lauda in the championship table.

In the event, both Regazzoni and Fittipaldi beat Lauda after he experienced shock absorber problems. But that third place was enough, and Lauda ended the season with 64.5 points to Fittipaldi's 45, having won five World Championship races - in Monaco, Belgium, France, Sweden and the USA - with the advantage of pole position in nine of the 14 Grand Prix.

The most complete driver of his era, Niki Lauda would survive a dreadful crash during the 1976 German Grand Prix at the Nürburgring, and overcome severe burns and lung damage to return to competition only six weeks later, only losing his world title to James Hunt by a single point. In 1977 he would regain his title, and win it again in 1984, by which time he had already founded Lauda Air, now Austria's second largest civil aviation company.

KIWI JOHN RACES TO MILE IMMORTALITY

One of the most accomplished athletes of his generation, New Zealander John Walker earned his immortality in Gothenburg on August 12 this year when he became the first man in history to run the mile in under 3 minutes 50 seconds.

It was the third time that the 25-year-old from Papakura had attracted headlines. In 1973, he was a member of the New Zealand team that had set a new world record for the 4 x 1,500m in Oslo, while in 1974, at the Commonwealth Games, he'd won a silver medal in the 1500m as race-winner Filbert Bayi set a new world record, and had also won a creditable bronze in the 800m.

Walker's achievement in Gothenburg (with a time of 3:49.4) would be matched by his 2,000m world record time of 4:51.1 in Oslo in 1976, just prior to taking the Olympic gold at 1,500m in Montreal.

John Walker

Although his subsequent Olympic career would be hit by boycotts and injuries, John Walker's consistency and appetite for racing would be rewarded in 1985 when he became the first man in history to run 100 sub four-minute miles.

After a remarkable two decades so near the top that a major mile, 1,500m, 3,000m or 5,000m final without his distinctive all-black strip and shoulder-length blond hair seemed a real rarity, John Walker finally called it a day when a fall in the 1990 Commonwealth Games ended his dreams of capping his career with a gold in front of an adoring Auckland crowd.

He now breeds horses near Auckland. And nobody would bet that he doesn't still pace himself against some of his charges...!

JULY 11

Terracotta Army Unearthed In China

ONE OF THE MOST REMARKABLE discoveries of all time was made today when Chinese archaeologists reported that a 6,000-strong 'terracotta army' had been uncovered by peasants looking for water near the tomb of the first Ch'in Emperor in north-western China, 2,000 years after the craftsmen who created the figures were themselves walled up inside the tomb to maintain total secrecy about its contents.

The life-sized figures included warriors, chariots, spears and horses, all drawn up in battle formation. They had lain buried since the Emperor Ch'in Shih-huang-ti - who gave China its Western name – died in 206 BC. It was thought that the 'army' was a memorial to the force which Ch'in led across China in a drive to unify the country.

Ch'in was responsible for building the Great Wall of China – the only man-made structure visible from space – and for changing Chinese society from a system ruled by slave-owning lords to a form of feudalism. He was also responsible for law reforms and introducing a simplified system of weights and measures to aid Chinese trade with other nations.

JULY 1
'Tyrant' Amin Reprieves Briton

President Idi Amin, the military dictator of Uganda, today submitted to international pressure and reprieved 61-year-old Briton Denis Cecil Hills, who was under sentence of death for describing Amin as a 'tyrant' in a manuscript as yet unpublished.

The capricious dictator had previously indicated that he would not reprieve Hills unless British Foreign Secretary James Callaghan visited the Ugandan capital, Kampala, in person, and also questioned the safety of 700 other Britons living in Uganda.

Amin had ruled Uganda since seizing power from President Milton Obote in 1971. Regarded largely as a laughing stock by the West, he was nevertheless responsible for the deaths of hundreds of thousands of his own countrymen and women.

JULY 5
Arthur Ashe Takes Wimbledon Title

American tennis player Arthur Ashe, 32, today became the first black man in the history of the game to win the Men's Singles Championship at Wimbledon when he beat the odds-on favourite, Jimmy Connors, on the Centre Court. Ashe, who had led the US Davis Cup team between 1968 and 1972, would later become a top administrator in the game before contracting Aids from a blood transfusion during heart surgery. After going public and founding an Aids charity in the US, he would die in 1993.

The 1975 Ladies' Singles title went, more predictably, to American veteran and Wimbledon favourite Billie Jean King, who beat Australia's Evonne Cawley to gain her sixth Wimbledon Singles title – just one of the 20 she won during her illustrious career.

JULY 1
London Police Reveal PLO Hit-List

Scotland Yard detectives today revealed evidence that Palestinian terrorists had drawn up a 'hit-list' of leading Western public figures - showbiz impresario Bernard Delfont, store tycoon Lord Sainsbury and musician Yehudi Menuhin among them.

The list was discovered, along with firearms and hand-grenades, at the 'safe-house' which the terrorist known as 'Carlos' was using as a London hide-out.

Scotland Yard alerted French police in what became an international search to track down the killer who had known links with Palestinian terrorist organizations. He would not, however, be captured until 1995.

UK TOP 10 SINGLES

1: Tears On My Pillow
- Johnny Nash
2: Misty
- Ray Stevens
3: The Hustle
- Van McCoy
4: Have You Seen Her/Oh Girl
- The Chi-Lites
5: I'm Not In Love
- 10cc
6: Give A Little Love
- The Bay City Rollers
7: Disco Stomp
- Hamilton Bohannon
8: Eighteen With A Bullet
- Pete Wingfield
9: Barbados
Typically Tropical
10: Whispering Grass
- Windsor Davies & Don Estelle

33

DEPARTURES

Died this month:
2: James Robertson Justice, British film character actor *(Scott Of The Antarctic, Whiskey Galore, Doctor In The House, The Fast Lady,* etc), aged 70
15: Charles Weidman, American dancer, aged 73
19: Lefty Frizzell (William Orville Frizzell), US country music superstar, aged 47

JULY 19

US Greets USSR With Handshake In Space

EAST-WEST *DÉTENTE* was definitely in the air today when, in a historic moment, Soviet and US astronauts linked their spacecraft 140 miles above the Atlantic Ocean.

Three years in the planning, the Apollo-Soyuz Test Project (ASTP) saw the separate *Apollo* and *Soyuz* teams join forces for two days with a symbolic handshake through the hatches of their respective spacecraft.

The two three-man crews, led by Tom Stafford and Alexei Leonov, spent the two days carrying out experiments, appearing on TV broadcasts and sharing what amounted to everyday life in space, including their meals.

Later, the two spacecraft flew in close formation together, each making observations of the earth and the sun to their respective mission controls.

JULY 19

Horror Stories From Cambodia

The little news that managed to filter through the communications blackout in Cambodia was not good. Refugees who evaded the tight security net to reach the safety of Thailand today brought with them horrifying stories of human rights abuses – city-dwellers herded into the countryside, yoked to ploughs and made to do the work of water buffalo.

According to the refugees, these slave labourers worked from dawn till dusk, with no tools and only a single bowl of rice to sustain them. Many were dying from malnutrition and physical abuse, and thousands more had been executed by Pol Pot's Khmer Rouge soldiers.

JULY 29

Absent Gowon Deposed By Nigerian Coup

Yakubu Danjuma Gowon, the man who led Nigeria's government during the country's civil war with Biafran rebels between 1967 and 1970, was today deposed in a bloodless coup while out of the country attending a meeting of the Organization of African Unity in Uganda.

A career army officer, Gowon became the Nigerian Army's Chief of Staff after a coup in January 1966. After the Nigerian Government's victory in 1970, he initiated a policy of reconciliation and extensive reconstruction. However, anticipated oil revenue did not match expenditure and he paid the penalty.

JULY 30

A Hoffa You Can't Refuse

Jimmy Hoffa, America's most powerful labour union leader, disappeared from a Detroit restaurant tonight, never to be seen again.

The charismatic Hoffa, born in 1913, had been largely responsible for creating the International Brotherhood of Teamsters, a major trade union for freight-haulers. After its expulsion from the American trades union organization, the AFL-CIO in 1957, he was largely unchallenged in how he ran the Teamsters.

Convicted of fraud, nobbling juries and looting pension funds, he was behind bars for four years before President Nixon commuted his term. The mystery of his disappearance (he was officially declared dead in 1982) cemented his place in mythology and Hollywood eventually moved in. Danny DeVito would direct a movie version of his life in 1992.

35

AUGUST 1

Helsinki Agreement Confirms Human Rights Pact

ALTHOUGH THE HELSINKI ACCORD - which was finally signed in the Finnish capital today - would largely be overtaken in the 1990s by perestroika (the Gorbachev-inspired policy of greater openness) and the break-up of the Soviet bloc, at the time of its signing it represented a major breakthrough in East-West relations.

The agreement, which was the direct result of the multinational Conference on Security and Co-operation in Europe, was signed by 33 European countries, together with the US and Canada. It balanced a Western recognition of Soviet power in Eastern Europe with human rights guarantees for those living there.

For the first time, the Soviet regime was pledged to uphold the civil rights and free movement of people and ideas across national frontiers. Present to sign the Accord, Soviet leader Leonid Brezhnev was clearly unwell. His voice slurred as he read from a prepared speech, he said, 'No one should try to dictate to other peoples the manner in which they ought to conduct their internal affairs'.

AUGUST 4

British Rock Legends Set To Crumble?

Three major British rock institutions were shaken to their foundations this month – and most of the trouble centred round their flamboyant lead singers.

Led Zeppelin frontman Robert Plant was today hospitalized with his wife after a car crash in Greece, and both would be flown back to Britain for treatment. Thankfully, both would recover fully.

Art-rockers Genesis were to lose their singer, Peter Gabriel. He claimed the need to 'absorb a wide variety of influences'.

Meanwhile, The Faces' future looked bleak as Rod Stewart's solo album, *Atlantic Crossing* - recorded with the cream of US session men - took off for the top of the charts. With guitarist Ron Wood having been poached by The Rolling Stones, the likelihood of the group – born from the ashes of 1960s hitmakers The Small Faces – recording or touring together again seemed highly remote.

36

AUGUST 11
Labour Take British Leyland Into State Control

The ailing British Leyland company - the only major British-owned motor manufacturer, and producer of Austin, Morris, Jaguar and Rover cars - passed into government ownership today. It was, said the Labour government, the only way the company could survive. Subject of a damning report by Lord Ryder earlier this year, BL was said to need an injection of £1,400 million ($2,800m) capital to ensure its survival. The only way the government would do that was if management control was handed to the National Enterprise Board. The chairman of the NEB? Lord Ryder.

AUGUST 19
Just Not Cricket As Vandals Spoil Test Pitch

The last day's play in the five-day Test Match due to be played today in Leeds between England and Australia was abandoned - not for the usual reasons of poor light or foul weather, but because the pitch had been dug up by a group campaigning for the release of jailed London cab-driver George Davis, victim of what they believed was a miscarriage of justice.

The wicket at Yorkshire's Headingley headquarters, which four days previously had been the scene of Middlesex spin-bowler Phil Edmonds' impressive début (he took five Australian wickets for just 17 runs), was doomed unplayable after what cricket fans still regard as an act of 'sacrilege'.

The subject of the protest, Davis, was later released, although in September 1977 he was arrested again, for his part in a bank raid, and subsequently sentenced to 15 years for robbery.

UK TOP 10 SINGLES

1: Barbados
- Typically Tropical
2: Can't Give You Anything (But My LOve)
- The Stylistics
3: If You Think You Know How To Love Me
- Smokey
4: Give A Little Love
- The Bay City Rollers
5: Jive Talkin'
- The Bee Gees
6: The Last Farewell
- Roger Whittaker
7: It's Been So Long
- George McCrae
8: Sealed With A Kiss
- Brian Hyland
9: It's In His Kiss
- Linda Lewis
10: Blanket On The Ground
- Billie Jo Spears

DEPARTURES

Died this month:
8: Cannonball Adderley, US modern jazz pioneer, alto sax player
10: Dmitri Shostakovich, Russian composer *(see main story)*
15: Sheikh Mujibur Rahman, Bangladeshi visionary *(see main story)*
21: Sam McGhee, US country music guitarist
27: Haile Selassie, Emperor of Ethiopia *(see main story)*
29: Éamonn de Valéra, Irish statesman, Prime Minister 1932-48, 1951-4, 1957-9, President 1959-73 *(see main story)*

AUGUST 29

De Valéra, Supreme Irish Patriot, Dies

MORE THAN ANY OTHER MAN in the 20th century, Éamonn de Valéra worked tirelessly for the people of Ireland and the country that he loved. It was even on his mind at the end when, on his deathbed today, he said, 'All my life I have done my best for Ireland. Now, I am ready to go'.

Born in the US in 1882, of a Spanish father and an Irish mother, de Valéra was taken to Ireland at the age of two. As a young man he became involved in the Irish Volunteers (a forerunner of the IRA), taking part in the Easter Uprising of 1916.

Sixteen of the rebel leaders were executed for their part in the rebellion but de Valéra escaped with a life sentence, of which he served just one year because of his American citizenship. A one-time President of Sinn Féin, he broke away to found Fianna Fáil in 1926, and it was as its leader that he would serve four separate periods as Irish Prime Minister. At the age of 76, he was elected President.

Always opposed to the division of Ireland, he was not a man of violence, fostering strong links between the Catholic Church and the state and banning the IRA. He succeeded in keeping Ireland neutral during World War II and withdrew Eire from the British Commonwealth in 1949.

AUGUST 15

Bangladeshi Coup Leaves Leader Dead

Sheikh Mujibur Rahman - known as the 'Father of Bangladesh' for his leadership of the Awami League's fight to create the independent republic of Bangladesh in 1971 - was murdered today during an army coup. His wife, two eldest sons and other members of his family were also killed by soldiers.

Born of a well-to-do family in East Bengal, Rahman persistently fought for Bengali rights both during British colonial rule and, after 1947, within the new nation of Pakistan. In 1949 he co-founded the moderately socialist Awami (People's) League, which became Pakistan's first opposition party.

He suffered several spells in jail as a result of his support for the struggle of the Bengalis for equality with the western Punjabis. Civil war broke out in 1971, and when India intervened on the side of East Pakistan a rapid victory was achieved for East Pakistan which became Bangladesh.

The huge problems faced by Rahman in attempting to transform the hopelessly poor country of Bangladesh seemed insurmountable, and it was when he assumed the powers of a dictator in 1975 that the coup was prompted.

AUGUST 10

Shostakovich Takes Final Bow

The Soviet Union's most famous modern composer, Dmitri Shostakovich, died at the age of 68 today, victim of a long-standing heart condition. His music achieved no mean compromise, having a foot firmly in the traditional and modernist music camps.

Shostakovich also trod a precarious line in his homeland, where Stalinist restrictions on formalistic and bourgeois music meant that he was able to produce nothing but film-scores and patriotic compositions for the five years up to Stalin's death in 1953.

Hailed by many as the greatest composer of the twentieth century, Shostakovich's greatest achievement was probably the survival of his genius in a system not known for its desire to foster individualism and creativity.

AUGUST 27

The Last Ethiopian Emperor

Haile Selassie, the last Emperor of Ethiopia who was deposed in 1974 in a left-wing military coup, died today at the age of 83, while still under house arrest. Although he had been unable to solve Ethiopia's complicated social problems, his half-century of rule had seen many advances for the country in which he instituted modernist reforms in many areas of public life – the law, education, the economy and administration – and abolished feudalism and slavery.

He was also responsible, in 1963, for the creation of the Organization of African Unity, which had been successful in mediating in a number of border disputes in the continent.

QUEEN'S RHAPSODY IS THE REAL THING!

It's almost impossible to overstate the importance of Queen's single *Bohemian Rhapsody*, which lodged at No 1 in the UK charts for seven weeks at the end of this year, and did likewise all over Europe.

Although the group - singer Freddie Mercury, guitarist Brian May, bassist John Deacon and drummer Roger Taylor - had enjoyed previous hits with *Seven Seas Of Rhye* and *Killer Queen* in 1974 and *Now I'm Here* earlier in 1975, *Bohemian Rhapsody* would prove the point at which a successful and respected group became international superstars capable of building and maintaining a 15-year career at the top of their very competitive profession.

At almost six minutes long, *Bohemian Rhapsody* was twice the length of average singles, and while radio stations had played The Beatles' seven-minutes-plus *Hey Jude* in 1968, no one believed that a relatively unknown group could get away with it. They did.

The song also broke every rule in the book for style, stopping and starting, and going off at often bizarre musical and lyrical tangents. It also came accompanied by what was arguably the world's first pop video, like the single, a challenging mass of often-conflicting images and moods.

Although the more rigid US Top 40 radio formats would limit airplay for *Bohemian Rhapsody* and it would only sneak into the lower half of the US Top 20 in mid-1976 as a result, it would achieve the status as one of rock's most enduring anthems and return to the top of the British charts in 1991 in the aftermath of Freddie Mercury's death from AIDS.

ABBA START TO ROLL

Although they'd enjoyed a huge international hit with their 1974 Eurovision Song Contest winner *Waterloo* and scored a pair of medium-sized successes with the follow-ups *Ring Ring* and *I Do I Do I Do*, no one really believed that the Swedish quartet ABBA would prove to be one of the biggest-selling and most popular recording acts of the next seven years.

First signs that Benny, Björn, Agnetha and Anni-Frid were going to enjoy more than their allotted five minutes of fame came in September when *SOS* raced up every major European chart. By December, when *Mamma Mia* became an even bigger smash, even the most hardened cynics were admitting that something remarkable was going on, and that ABBA had to be taken seriously.

By the time ABBA called it a day in 1983, they'd put together an unbroken run of 23 hit singles, no fewer than nine of them reaching No 1 in Britain and most of them making the top five. In the process, they managed at one stage to out-perform the Volvo car company as Sweden's biggest export earner!

TAMMY STANDS BY HER MAN THROUGH D-I-V-O-R-C-E

Two of the most unexpected hits of this year in Britain were Tammy Wynette's *Stand By Your Man* and *D-I-V-O-R-C-E*, both of which had been No 1 in the US country charts in 1968 but were re-released and re-promoted in Britain after Radio One DJ John Peel included them in his late night show and was deluged with requests for more.

Queen

Ironically, by the time the 33-year-old singer (real name Virginia Wynette Pugh) was packing her bags to visit Britain for TV and live performances, she was in the throes of her second divorce - this one to country superstar George Jones - and would in fact clock up five marriages and four divorces by the mid-1990s!

Tammy was first married at the age of 17 and was a divorced mother of three by the age of 20. Chasing her dreams, she moved to Nashville, was 'discovered' by top producer Billy Sherrill (with whom she wrote *Stand By Your Man* during a 20-minute recording session break) and began to make a string of million-selling records.

Her British and European breakthrough proved the icing on a very big cake as Tammy continued to defy all trends in the US and racked up even more huge hits through the 1970s and 1980s while also spending time as a patient at the Betty Ford Clinic to shake off a drug dependency.

The publication of her frank autobiography (guess the title!) in 1982 would lead to a successful movie. Tammy entered the 1990s back at the top of the British charts as a surprise guest on *Justified And Ancient* by the avant-garde rock group KLF, and a 1993 album with the self-explanatory title *Tears Of Fire: The 25th Anniversary Collection* which featured duets with a number of major country stars including ex-No 2, George Jones.

SEPTEMBER 18

Kidnap Victim Patty Faces Robbery Charges

The strange saga of Patty Hearst, the US publishing empire heiress kidnapped from her San Francisco home 19 months ago by an urban guerrilla group known as the Symbionese Liberation Army (SLA), took another bizarre twist today when she was charged, along with SLA members, with the armed robbery of a Californian bank.

Seized by the SLA in February 1974, the 20-year-old's father, publishing tycoon Randolph Hearst, initially funded a food relief programme for the San Francisco poor and homeless to ensure her safety. But when a badly disguised Patty was filmed by security cameras taking part in an SLA bank robbery, the FBI stopped looking for a captive and added her to a list of wanted fugitives.

Despite her pleas that she'd been brainwashed and coerced into joining the SLA, Patty would be sentenced to seven years in prison, a sentence commuted by President Jimmy Carter in 1979. Patty would later marry the private detective assigned to protect her.

SEPTEMBER 8

Scottish Captain Bremner In Life Ban Row

Billy Bremner, 32-year-old captain of Scotland's soccer team, was today given a life ban from playing for his country after an alleged post-match brawl in a Copenhagen nightclub. Four other players - Arthur Graham, Joe Harper, Pat McCluskey and Willie Young - were also accused of incidents which followed Scotland's single-goal victory over Denmark on September 3 in the European Championship. All received the same sentence.

Despite his protestations of innocence, Bremner - who'd been capped 54 times for his country - was banned without being given the chance to defend himself to the Scottish committee which condemned him and the others.

The ban would mark a downturn in Bremner's career. A year later he was transferred from the mighty English First Division champions, Leeds United, to the relatively lowly Second Division side, Hull City. While he would later return to Leeds for a brief spell as manager, Bremner's top-level playing days were over.

SEPTEMBER 6

Tennis Ace Navratilova Defects To West

MARTINA NAVRATILOVA, the 18-year-old Czech-born tennis player who'd emerged as one of the sport's most exciting new international talents during the past two years, today asked to be allowed to stay permanently in the US, citing interference by the Czech sporting authorities as her principal reason for seeking political asylum. Temporary approval was given while her case was considered.

A move to the West was bound to increase Navratilova's earning potential, since players remaining behind the Iron Curtain had their winnings paid direct to the state. While their relative freedom to travel abroad, and the 'perks' granted to successful players, made them far more fortunate than most of their compatriots, many sports stars rightly objected to the bulk of their considerable earnings being pocketed by a regime most of them actively disliked.

Navratilova would subsequently be granted permission to stay in the US. However, she was initially so overcome by the abundance of American life that she developed eating problems which kept championship success out of reach for two years. In the late 1970s new found self-discipline on and off the court began to pay dividends, and she would go on to win a string of top titles throughout the following decades to earn well-deserved superstar status.

UK TOP 10 SINGLES

1: Sailing
- Rod Stewart
2: The Last Farewell
- Roger Whittaker
3: Moonlighting
- Leo Sayer
4: Summertime City
- Mike Batt
5: Funky Moped/Magic Roundabout
- Jasper Carrott
6: A Child's Prayer
- Hot Chocolate
7: Can't Give You Anything (But My Love)
- The Stylistics
8: That's The Way (I Like It)
- KC & The Sunshine Band
9: I'm On Fire
- 5000 Volts
10: Heartbeat
- Showaddywaddy

DEPARTURES

Died this month:
4: Wally Barnes, UK football player, former Arsenal star, aged 55

SEPTEMBER 17

Nicholson Goes Cuckoo, Thanks To Kirk

The film on everybody's lips this month, *One Flew Over The Cuckoo's Nest,* was one of Hollywood's most remarkable 'sleepers', having taken 14 years to get off the ground. Starring Jack Nicholson as McMurphy, an anarchic mental hospital inmate who locks horns with Matron Ratched, played by Louise Fletcher, the film was based on a novel by American author Ken Kesey first published in the early sixties. Kirk Douglas, who had played the male lead in a New York stage version, had been so impressed by the story that he bought the film rights, but could never get the finance to bring it to the big screen. His son, Michael, took them over and was now reaping the rewards. Translated to the screen by Milos Forman, the notably anti-authoritarian Czech-born director, *One Flew Over The Cuckoo's Nest* was immediately tipped for top award honours for Forman, Nicholson - a Best Actor Oscar nominee for the past two years - and Fletcher.

SEPTEMBER 28

Basque Terrorists Executed

Sentenced to death by garrotting in a Spanish court last month, today's execution of five Basque terrorists by that barbaric method sparked a wave of international demonstrations at Spanish embassies, condemnation by world civil rights and judiciary bodies, and the recall of their Ambassadors in Madrid by Britain, Norway, the Netherlands, Denmark and both East and West Germany.

The following day, Spanish police would shoot six people taking part in a mass demonstration against the executions, outraging international opinion further.

The five, who had been convicted of killing two Spanish policemen, were said to be members of ETA, the guerrilla movement seeking separation from Spain for their mountainous region. Encompassing four Spanish and three French provinces, the Basque region boasted its own language and distinct cultural identity. ETA's terrorist campaign would continue unabated until 1980, when the Basques were granted what amounted to home rule.

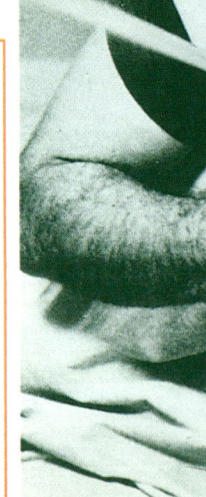

SEPTEMBER 5

President Ford Cheats Death Twice

LUCK WAS A LADY to US President Gerald Ford today, when he escaped what would be only the first of two attempted assassinations this month. The identity of today's would-be killer brought an uncomfortable memory of the darker side of the American dream - the mass killer Charles Manson and his so-called Family, whose drug-crazed marauding in 1968 and 1969 ended with the horrific murders of the pregnant actress Sharon Tate and a group of friends, and a wealthy Los Angeles couple, the LaBiancas.

The woman, who was wrestled to the ground by security men after pointing a loaded gun at the President, was Lynette 'Squeaky' Fromme, one of the Manson Family jailed for the Tate-LaBianca murders in 1970, but once again at liberty. Her failed attack took place during the President's visit to Sacramento, the Californian capital.

On September 22, in San Francisco, another woman 45-year-old Sara Jane Moore - actually managed to fire a shot at President Ford as he left an hotel. Fortunately, she missed and was quickly subdued by police and security staff.

Both would be found guilty of attempted murder when they came to trial in December, and both would be sentenced to life imprisonment.

OCT

OCTOBER 23

London Cancer Specialist Killed As Ulster Explodes

Professor Gordon Fairley, an internationally renowned cancer specialist, was killed today, the innocent victim of an IRA car bomb attack on one of his neighbours, the Conservative MP Hugh Fraser.

The blast which shook the South London suburb came two weeks after IRA bombers had killed one person and injured 20 others outside the Central London underground Green Park station to resume their terror campaign on the British mainland.

The civil war in Ulster also reached a new crescendo as a hard-line Protestant organization, the Ulster Volunteer Force (UVF), began a wave of revenge killings on October 2. Eleven people died in UVF attacks, although four UVF terrorists were killed when a car bomb exploded prematurely.

As Republicans accused the UVF of trying to provoke further IRA violence, Ulster Secretary Merlyn Rees banned the UVF. By the end of the month, internal differences within the IRA had deteriorated so much that the October 31 fatal shooting of Provisional IRA leader Seamus McCusker in Belfast was acknowledged as the work of the Official IRA.

OCTOBER 3

Spaghetti House Hostages Freed

One of the most bizarre hostage dramas ever seen in Britain ended peacefully today when seven Italians were released by their captors - a gang of bungling burglars - from the Spaghetti House restaurant in Knightsbridge, Central London. The thwarted robbers then gave themselves up to the armed police surrounding the building.

The saga began on September 28 when the robbery gang hit the Spaghetti House at 2 am, expecting to find only the manager still there. Instead, there were seven staff in the restaurant and, when one of the workers kicked the night's takings under a counter, the robbers panicked and took everyone hostage.

46

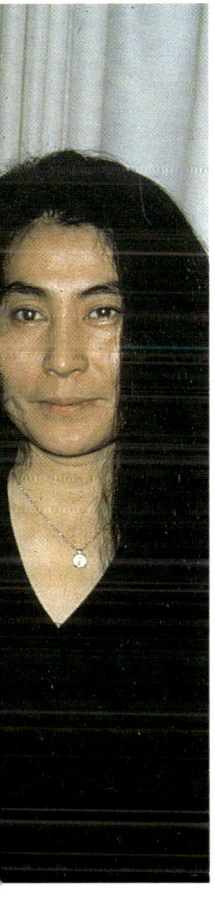

OCTOBER 7

Lennon Stays In His American Dream

BRITISH MUSICIAN and ex-Beatle John Lennon won his four-year battle to remain in the US today, just days before his 35th birthday, when three judges in the US Court of Appeals decided against the Immigration Service's decision to disallow an extension of Lennon's stay because of a British conviction for marijuana possession seven years earlier.

The appeal judges concurred with a recent *New York Post* editorial, which stated, 'The crime for which John Lennon was convicted in London in 1968 would not even land him in a New York jail', and described Lennon's battle as 'testimony to his faith in this American dream'.

Lennon, who retired from public life to raise his son, Sean - who was coincidentally born on October 9, to make this a memorable month for him and his wife, the Japanese-born artist, Yoko Ono - would remain an American resident until his murder in November 1980, at the hands of crazed fan Mark Chapman.

OCTOBER 20

Politician Reagan Takes National Stage

Former Hollywood actor Ronald Reagan unexpectedly entered the 1976 US presidential election race today when he announced his intention of seeking the Republican Party nomination. He'd moved into politics as Governor of California, but it was his humble, man-in-the-street image which many thought gave him credibility in the post-Watergate era.

Commentators were quick to write Reagan off as a complete non-starter. He was, for instance, already 64-years-old. Worse, he was a divorced man. Worst of all, he was an ex-actor.

They appeared correct when Reagan's 1976 bid failed. However, when he did become President in 1980, by then aged 69, he would be the oldest man ever to take over the Oval Office, and he would successfully seek a second term before being succeeded by his deputy, George Bush.

UK TOP 10 SINGLES

1: Hold Me Close
- David Essex
2: I Only Have Eyes For You
- Art Garfunkel
3: There Goes My First Love
- The Drifters
4: It's Time For Love
- The Chi-Lites
5: Una Paloma Blanca
- Jonathan King
6: Who Loves You
- The Four Seasons
7: SOS
- Abba
8: Scotch On The Rocks
- Band Of The Black Watch
9: Feelings
  Morris Albert
10: Funky Moped/Magic Roundabout
- Jasper Carrott

47

ARRIVALS

Born this month:
8: Laura Vasquez, Australian TV actress (*Home And Away*)

DEPARTURES

Died this month:
1: Al Jackson, US soul-rock drummer (Booker T & The MGs), aged 39
22: Arnold Joseph Toynbee, British historian (*A Study Of History*), former journalist and Professor of Byzantine and Modern Greek Studies, London University
30: Guy Mollet, French politician (Secretary-General of the French Socialist Party 1946-68, head of French coalition government 1956-7), aged 69

OCTOBER 10

Burton And Taylor Remarry

Film stars Elizabeth Taylor and Richard Burton were married for the second time today in a remote village in the African country of Botswana. Ever since the couple played opposite one another in the spectacular Hollywood extravaganza, *Cleopatra,* in 1963, their tempestuous relationship had been conducted more or less in the public eye, with gossip columnists eager to pass on details of their on-off-on again marriage, their many rows and their jet-set lifestyle.

Sadly, this much less public attempt at reconciliation was to fail. Taylor would make several more marriages after her second to Burton, who also went on to remarry.

OCTOBER 30
Dutch Elm Disease Kills 6.5 Million

According to a report published in London today by the Forestry Commission, the deadly Dutch Elm Disease was changing the face of rural Britain for ever. Spread by a fungus, it had already killed more than 6.5 million of the distinctive trees which were so much a part of the British landscape.

First discovered in France at the end of World War I, it began to take hold in Britain during the late 1960s. After taking hold in southern England, it was reportedly gaining ground in the North. No cure was possible for infected trees, although scientists were known to be trying to develop a disease-resistant variety.

OCTOBER 9
Nobel Peace Prize For Dissident Sakharov

THE RUSSIAN SCIENTIST and human rights campaigner, Dr Andrei Sakharov, was today announced as this year's recipient of the prestigious Nobel Peace Prize, in recognition of his brave crusade for nuclear disarmament and democracy in the Soviet Union.

Recognized internationally for his work in nuclear physics and decorated three times as a Hero of Socialist Labour, Sakharov – who had been called the Father of the Soviet H-bomb – displeased Communist Party bosses when he protested at their intention to violate the international Nuclear Test-Ban Treaty in 1961.

A tireless defender of civil liberties, the 54-year-old also publicly criticized the Soviet Government's record on the treatment of political prisoners and dissidents. From 1980 to 1986 he would be sentenced to internal exile from Moscow, in the city of Gorky. His freedom restored by President Gorbachev, Sakharov remained a vigorous critic of government policies, and would be elected to the Congress of People's Deputies in 1989.

OCTOBER 27
Springsteen Calls Time On Hype

In an unprecedented move, the sober US current-affairs magazines *Time* and *Newsweek* both put Bruce Springsteen, the rock music sensation of the season, on their front covers today. The singer-songwriter and his backing group, The E-Street Band, had taken the US by storm with the album and single *Born To Run*, the former reaching the US top three.

Unfortunately, the hype would initially rebound on the artist, most notably when a quote by journalist Jon Landau ('I saw rock 'n'roll's future – and its name is Bruce Springsteen') was emblazoned on huge billboard posters by Springsteen's record company. A furious Springsteen would tear down as many of the posters as he could before reconciling himself to the hyperbole and getting down to the business of proving himself a lasting talent.

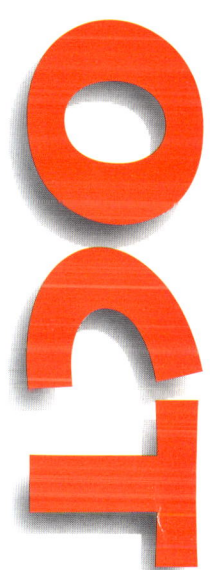

49

NOVEMBER 20
GENERAL FRANCO - STEEL FIST IN A METAL GLOVE

By definition, dictators are people (invariably men) absolutely convinced in their beliefs, one of which is that anyone who does not unconditionally share their beliefs is a danger to be suppressed or, in extreme cases, ruthlessly eliminated. General Francisco Franco, the supreme dictator of Spain for 40 years, met that definition in full, retaining his single-minded credo until his death today at the age of 82.

Born into a naval family, Franco was educated at the Toledo Infantry Academy and, on graduating in 1910, served until 1927 in Morocco, where he distinguished himself in action against Arab nationalists seeking a break from Spain. Promoted to full general in 1927, he was appointed principal of the Saragossa Military Academy.

Keeping clear of politics, he became rabidly anti-communist in 1934 when he was called on to suppress a miners' 'soviet' and did so with ruthless efficiency and brutality. A confused political situation in 1935-36 saw him made Chief of the General Staff, the post he held when, in January 1936, he was Spain's representative at the London funeral of King George V.

Returning to take the post of Governor of the Canary Islands, he led the anti-socialist military revolt which sparked off the Spanish Civil War and was proclaimed *generalissimo* and head of state of Nationalist Spain - a newly-formed state which was almost immediately recognized by Adolf Hitler and Benito Mussolini, two like-minded fascists. Britain, France and the US would only recognize his government in 1939, when Franco's troops had finally emerged victorious in Spain's terrible and

bloody civil war by taking Barcelona and Madrid.

Despite his sympathy for Hitler and Mussolini, Franco maintained Spain's neutrality during World War II, and reinforced his own position - in the face of widespread international condemnation of his regime - by declaring himself *Caudillo* (head of state) for life, or until the monarchy he'd suspended in 1939 was restored.

Franco's steadfast refusal to amend or modernize Spain's increasingly corrupt political and administrative institutions, or to relax his absolute powers, inevitably led to serious unrest - especially among a generation of students who could see for themselves how their contemporaries in many other countries were dictating the pace of change. The Catholic Church also began to rankle at his rule, while Basque separatists turned to ever more violent methods to win independence from Spanish rule.

In 1969, Franco surprised many when he nominated Prince Juan Carlos - not the first in line to the long-deposed Borbon monarchy - to succeed him. That did in fact happen three weeks before Franco died, probably aware that the future king would liberate Spain from the restrictions Franco had installed and maintained throughout his long and repressive reign.

But those changes would not be any of his doing.

MAY 13
BOB WILLS - THE KING OF WESTERN SWING

While experts still haggle over whether or not James Robert Wills, who died today at his home in Texas at the age of 68, actually created the musical style known as western swing, no-one argues that he became and remains its most popular and inventive practitioner. Through his songs, his various excellent groups and his outstanding popularity with non-country fans in the 1930s, '40s and '50s, Bob Wills did as much, if not more than, almost any other artist to popularize country music with the huge pop audience.

The oldest of 10 children of a fiddle-playing father, Wills moved with his parents to Memphis, Texas when he was eight, playing fiddle only after he'd mastered the mandolin. He formed his first Bob Wills And His Texas Playboys group in 1933 after being sacked from his previous band job (for drinking) and moved to Oklahoma and the start of immense success via a radio show which was broadcast across the US.

Signed to Brunswick Records in 1935, Wills began a period of unrivalled popularity via records, syndicated radio shows and a residency at Cain's Academy in Tulsa. The musical mix of the band was formidable, containing as it did elements of jazz, blues, country ballads and a horns-and-fiddles blend which defied categorization.

In 1940 that blend crystalized in *San Antonio Rose*, the Wills song which, with Tommy Duncan's sweet vocals upfront, sold more than a million. Other Wills compositions which have become standards include *Faded Love, Take Me Back To Tulsa* and *Stay A Little Longer*.

With the US mobilizing for war in the wake of Pearl Harbor in 1942, Wills joined a number of his musicians in the services, but was discharged as medically unfit a year later. Basing himself in California, he spent the war years appearing as a guest on radio shows and making several films. The war over, he reformed The Texas Playboys as a smaller outfit, and while his audience remained loyal, Wills suffered doubts about his musical direction and increasing health problems.

In 1962, Wills had his first heart attack, fought back to return to the road, but in 1964 had a second more serious coronary which forced him to stop touring. Recording was still possible, however, and he continued to go into the studio regularly. In 1968 he was elected to the Country Music Hall of Fame, was honoured by the state of Texas in 1969, suffered a stroke the day after the celebrations, and it was not until 1972 that he reappeared on-stage, now in a wheelchair.

In December 1973, Wills attended his last recording session with many of the original Playboys. Although the unit recorded 27 songs in two days, Wills was too unwell to do much more than drop in. He suffered a massive stroke the next day and went into a two-year coma from which he never emerged.

It is a measure of his continued influence that a new album of Wills material recorded in 1993 by the group Asleep At The Wheel attracted guest appearances by many current country superstars who admitted a debt to him - including Willie Nelson, Dolly Parton, Garth Brooks, Merle Haggard, Lyle Lovett, Suzy Bogguss, George Strait and rock star Huey Lewis.

51

NOV

NOVEMBER 22

Franco Dies – Monarchy Returns To Spain

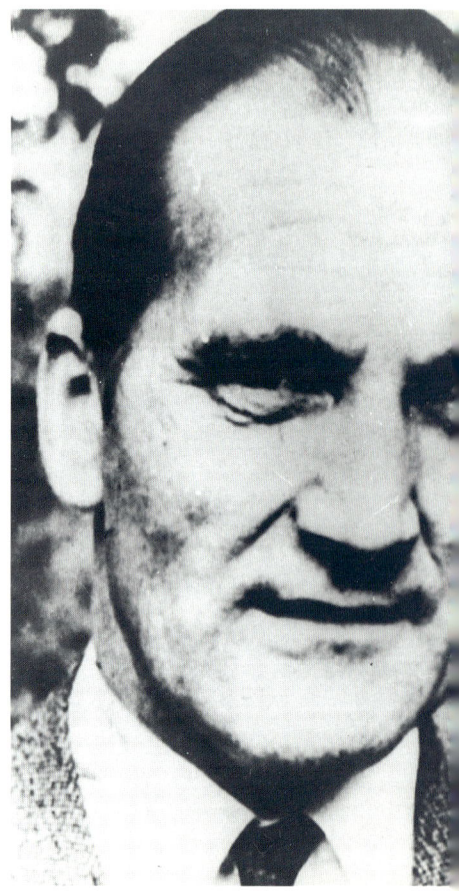

Don Juan Carlos Borbon y Borbon became King of Spain today, only two days after the sudden death of General Francisco Franco in Madrid, so returning the monarchy to a country which became a dictatorship under Franco in 1936.

The end of Franco's rule seemed likely to mark the beginning of an uncertain period, but his personally chosen and groomed successor indicated his hopes for the country when he promised 'far-reaching improvements' in his first official address to the Spanish parliament, the Cortes.

The new King, the first member of the royal family to sit on the throne since his grandfather, King Alfonso XIII, was forced into exile in 1931, announced a general amnesty to celebrate his accession. It proved an auspicious beginning to a period during which he would preside over Spain's transition from dictatorship to democracy.

Franco was buried in the 'Valley of the Fallen', the resting-place of Nationalist supporters who died in action during the Spanish Civil War of 1936-9.

NOVEMBER 7

IRA Frees Dutch Businessman Hostage

THIRTY-SIX DAYS OF TERROR ended today for Dutch industrialist Dr Tiede Herrema (pictured), snatched by IRA terrorists Marian Coyle and Eddie Gallagher on October 3 in a bid to force the Republic of Ireland government to release three IRA prisoners from prison.

While a massive nationwide hunt began for Dr Herrema and his captors, the Dublin authorities raised fears for the Dutchman's life when they refused to deal with Coyle and Gallagher.

Events had taken a dramatic turn on October 21 when it was confirmed that armed police and troops had surrounded a house in County Kildare. There followed a 19-day period of stand-off and negotiations, during which Dr Herrema had pleaded with police not to storm the house - he had a gun constantly at his head. Eventually realizing that their cause was lost, the IRA duo allowed their captive to walk free and unharmed before handing themselves over to face abduction charges.

NOVEMBER 3

Queen Opens North Sea Pipeline

The first British oil flowed ashore from the North Sea today when Queen Elizabeth II pressed a button to open the first pipeline from British Petroleum rigs in the Forties Field to the Grangemouth refinery on the Firth of Forth. Estimated to be capable of pumping 400,000 barrels of crude oil a day when in full production, the BP field was only one of a number of major British-developed oilfields reckoned to be worth around £200,000 million ($500,000m).

NOVEMBER 11

Civil War As Angola Gains Independence

Angola was at last made independent of Portuguese rule today, but within a fortnight was torn apart by a civil war which would make millions homeless and claim the lives of more than 40,000 in the first few months.

Three rival factions – the MPLA, UNITA and the FNLA – were being supplied by outside forces, South Africa, the US and the Soviet Union. Foreign involvement guaranteed that there would be no speedy solution for the strife-ridden country, and the fighting and suffering caused to the Angolan population was to be frequently in the news for the next sixteen years.

UK TOP 10 SINGLES

1: Space Oddity
- David Bowie
2: Love Is The Drug
- Roxy Music
3: D.I.V.O.R.C.E
- Tammy Wynette
4: Rhinestone Cowboy
- Glen Campbell
5: Love Hurts
- Jim Capaldi
6: You Sexy Thing
- Hot Chocolate
7: I Only Have Eyes For You
- Art Garfunkel
8: Imagine
- John Lennon
9: Hold Back The Night
- The Trammps
10: Blue Guitar
- Justin Hayward & John Lodge

DEPARTURES

Died this month:
6: Lionel Trilling, American novelist, aged 70
7: Cardinal John Heenan, Archbishop of Westminster, aged 70
20: General Francisco Franco, Spanish dictator 1936-75, aged 82 (*see main story*)
29: Graham Hill, British racing driver, world champion 1962 and 1968 (*see main story*)

NOVEMBER 11

Australia In Uproar As Brits Fire Prime Minister

THE UNACCEPTABLE IRON HAND of colonialism was exercised in Australia today by the Queen's official representative - the Governor-General, Sir John Kerr - when he dismissed the country's democratically elected Prime Minister, the left-wing Labour Party leader, Gough Whitlam (pictured), and threw Australia into a serious constitutional crisis.

Whitlam's Labour government had its hands tied a month earlier when the opposition Liberal and Country parties united in the Senate to reject its budget proposals. After weeks of acrimonious and increasingly rowdy stalemate, the Governor-General told Whitlam that he should resign and call an election if he couldn't arrange his funding.

When Whitlam refused, Sir John sacked him - an unprecedented move against an elected politician by an official whose duties are usually confined to the ceremonial. A shocked Australian public found themselves with a caretaker Liberal government headed by Malcolm Fraser. This became the elected government on December 13 when a general election was held, allowing the dust to settle.

NOVEMBER 29
Race Ace Hill Dies In Plane Crash

British racing driver Graham Hill – who gained widespread popularity in the 1960s for his exploits and victories on the world racing circuit – died today in an air crash at the age of 46, together with five members of the Lotus Grand Prix team.

The light aircraft which Hill was piloting came down in extreme weather and freezing fog near a small airfield at Elstree, close to Hill's north-west London home.

Twice winner of the world motor-racing championship, in 1962 with BRM and in 1968 with Lotus, Hill was returning from the South of France where he had been test-driving a car. He was survived by his wife and a son, Damon.

NOVEMBER 26
Holy Smoke! It's The Record-Burning Rev

Sparks flew today in Tallahassee, Florida, as the Rev Charles Boykin, pastor of the Lakeswood Baptist Church, and members of his congregation torched approximately $2,000 worth of rock records.

The Rev Boykin justified his unholy act of arson by quoting the statistic that 984 out of every 1,000 unmarried mothers became pregnant while rock music played in the background. Statisticians are still trying to establish the source of his assertion.

NOVEMBER 20
CIA 'Dirty Tricks' Exposed

A US Senate select committee investigating intelligence irregularities finally released its report on CIA links with foreign assassination attempts today in Washington DC.

Despite appeals by CIA director William Colby and a letter from President Ford asking him to suppress the report, Chairman Frank Church, a Democrat, released findings that the CIA had been responsible for planning the deaths of Fidel Castro in Cuba and Patrice Lumumba, Prime Minister of the Congo. Lumumba was, in fact, killed in 1961, reportedly while on the run from troops holding him prior to his trial for treason.

The committee also found evidence of CIA involvement in plots against Ngo Dinh Diem in South Vietnam and the Dominican Republic leader, General Rafael Trujillo, although they failed to find any involvement in the 1970 assassination of General Schneider of Chile.

DECEMBER 6
IRA Hold Couple In Balcombe Street Siege

A LONDON COUPLE – John (54) and Sheila Matthews (53) - became the centre of a terrorist drama tonight when four IRA men fleeing from police in a West End gun battle broke into the couple's Balcombe Street, Marylebone, council flat and used them as hostages to start what would become a six-day siege.

The gunmen, wanted for questioning about the murders of TV presenter and Guinness Book of Records compiler Ross McWhirter and a Metropolitan Police constable, demanded that they, and their hostages, be flown to the Republic of Ireland.

Those demands were firmly rejected by Detective Superintendent Peter Imbert who, during the six days of what the press immediately dubbed The Balcombe Street Siege, adopted a policy of negotiation while refusing to send in food. The siege ended without bloodshed and Mr and Mrs Matthews were released, shaken but unharmed. Peter Imbert would later rise to the rank of Police Commissioner.

DECEMBER 7
President Ford Visits China

US President Gerald Ford visited China for the first time today, planning to hold talks with Chairman Mao Tse-tung and so continue the process begun by President Richard Nixon at the beginning of the decade when diplomatic relationships between the US and China were first opened.

The presidential tour of the Far East also included the Philippines, where Ford was greeted by President Ferdinand Marcos, and confirmed the US decision to relinquish sovereignty over Clark Air Force Base – an installation forming an essential element of the American Pacific military presence – while retaining the right to control operations from it.

DECEMBER 8
Hurricane Bob Blows Big Apple Away

Folk-rock star Bob Dylan brought his long-running Rolling Thunder Revue to New York's Madison Square Garden tonight in a gigantic *Night Of The Hurricane* benefit show. The beneficiary was boxer Rubin 'Hurricane' Carter, whose apparently unjust incarceration for murder would be recounted in song on Dylan's forthcoming album *Desire*. Among those gathered in Carter's honour were fellow pugilist Muhammad Ali and singer Roberta Flack, as well as the all-star band Dylan himself headed. Carter came to the concert, if only via an amplified phone call to the stage, and the event raised some $100,000 towards the legal bills of Carter and alleged accomplice John Artis. Despite Dylan's efforts, Carter's conviction was never overturned.

DECEMBER 3
Cancer: Diet Is To Blame, Say Missionaries

Early evidence that cancer may have dietary causes was dismissed in London today by Britain's Flour Advisory Bureau as 'unjustified and inaccurate'. Even the *British Medical Journal* took the view that the evidence was 'circumstantial'.

Now a widely accepted fact, the cause and effect relationship between what we eat and the incidence of cancer was first noted by two missionaries, Denis Burkitt and Hubert Trowell, who attributed the low incidence of bowel disease in native Africans to their diet, which contained few refined foods such as white sugar and flour.

At the same time, American scientists issued a 300-page report which implicated fat, alcohol, pollution and vitamin deficiencies in the development of several varieties of cancer.

UK TOP 10 SINGLES

1: Bohemian Rhapsody
- Queen
2: You Sexy Thing
- Hot Chocolate
3: Trail Of The Lonesome Pine
- Laurel and Hardy with The Avalon Boys
4: Na Na Is The Saddest Word
- The Stylistics
5: Money Honey
- The Bay City Rollers
6: Let's Twist Again
- Chubby Checker
7: All Around My Hat
- Steeleye Span
8: I Believe In Father Christmas
- Greg Lake
9: Happy To Be On An Island In The Sun
- Demis Roussos
10: Show Me You're A Woman
- Mud

DEPARTURES

Died this month:

4: Hannah Arendt, German philosopher, aged 69

12: William Wellman, US film director and writer (*A Star Is Born, The Ox Bow Incident,* etc), aged 79

17: Theodore 'Hound Dog' Taylor, US blues guitarist, singer, aged 59

21: William Lundigan, US radio/movie/TV actor (*The Sea Hawk, Inferno,* etc), aged 61

25: Bernard Herrmann, US Academy Award-winning film composer (*Citizen Kane, All That Money Can Buy, The Trouble With Harry, Vertigo, Psycho, Fahrenheit 451, Taxi Driver,* etc), aged 64

DECEMBER 4

Moluccans Attack Consulate In Amsterdam

EUROPE APPEARED TO BE ONE HUGE terrorist target this month as a series of dramatic confrontations left the populations of Austria, Britain and Holland wondering if there would ever be an end to the apparently unending round of bomb attacks and hostage seizures which had become the most common weapons of so-called freedom fighters.

The first capital city to have the dubious honour of attracting world headlines today was Amsterdam, where seven armed dissidents from the former Dutch colony of South Molucca today brought their cause - for independence from their new Indonesian masters - to the mother country.

A raid on the Indonesian Consulate began what would become a 16-day siege as the Moluccans held 25 hostages at gunpoint to publicize their claims. There was only one fatality, when a hostage jumped to his death from a window. Otherwise, tension was so slight that a psychiatrist was eventually able to persuade the Moluccans to give in without further bloodshed (pictured).

Two Dutch commuters were less fortunate, however, on December 12 when another group of Moluccans hijacked their train. They were killed when caught in gunfire during the hijack. Like their compatriots in Amsterdam, the terrorists were persuaded to surrender. Their actions did little to help relations between native Dutch people and the 40,000 Moluccans estimated to live in Holland.

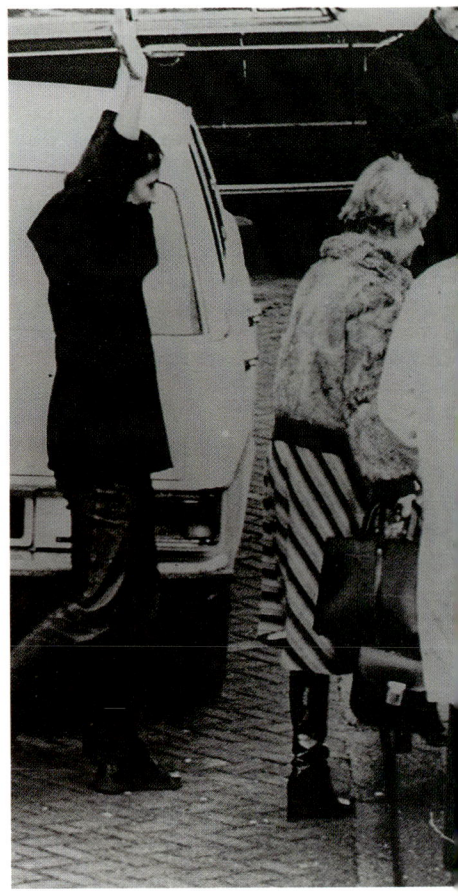

DECEMBER 7
Two-Time Pulitzer Winner Wilder Dies

America lost a native writer who made history when Thornton Wilder, a teacher by profession, died today at the age of 78. He received his historic second Pulitzer Prize in 1938 with his best-known play, *Our Town,* the first having been awarded in 1927 for his philosophical novel *The Bridge Of San Luis Rey.*

Less well known than these achievements, perhaps, is the fact that his two plays *The Merchant Of Yonkers* and *The Matchmaker* were later fused and adapted to become, in 1963, the hit musical comedy *Hello Dolly!*

DECEMBER 22
OPEC Summit Held To Ransom

The last incident to impose one country's problems on another came today in the Austrian capital, Vienna, when Palestinian terrorists took a number of OPEC (Organization of Petroleum-Exporting Countries) ministers hostage after killing three officials attending a summit.

The gunmen, who were believed to be led by the notorious South American hitman 'Carlos', demanded that Palestine receive a share of oil industry profits. The six terrorists also wounded eight people as they broke into the summit, holding 11 oil ministers and 59 others hostage to back their demands.

Wishing to avoid further loss of life, the Austrian Government allowed the gunmen and their hostages to fly to Algiers where, during a seven-hour stopover, the terrorists finally surrendered their arms. They were not held by the Algerians.

DECEMBER 24
Jim Fixes It For Xmas

British disc jockey Jimmy Savile tonight began a long-running association with the upper reaches of the TV ratings when he presented the first edition of his show, *Jim'll Fix It*. Its début appearance resulted in six million viewers tuning into the Christmas Eve show, with audiences peaking at a staggering 19.2 million in 1980.
The show's brilliantly simple concept was to let people's dreams come true – and the cigar-smoking Savile, who would be knighted for his charity work in 1990, more than fitted the bill as the genial host. As light entertainment went it didn't get much lighter, but Savile and the show rapidly became a British institution.

YOUR 1975 HOROSCOPE

Unlike most Western horoscope systems which group astrological signs into month-long periods based on the influence of 12 constellations, the Chinese believe that those born in the same year of their calendar share common qualities, traits and weaknesses with one of 12 animals - Rat, Ox, Tiger, Rabbit, Dragon, Snake, Horse, Sheep, Monkey, Rooster, Dog or Pig.

They also allocate the general attributes of five natural elements - Earth, Fire, Metal, Water, Wood - and an overall positive or negative aspect to each sign to summarize its qualities.

If you were born between January 23, 1974 and February 10, 1975, you are a Tiger. As this book is devoted to the events of 1975, let's take a look at the sign which governs those born between February 11 that year and January 30, 1976 - The Year of The Rabbit:

THE RABBIT
FEBRUARY 11, 1975 - JANUARY 30, 1976
ELEMENT: METAL ASPECT: (-)

Rabbits are peace-loving creatures who hate anything to do with violence, brutality and war, will avoid physical conflict throughout their lives and are committed pacifists. These traits make them good negotiators and communicators of ideas, always compromising to a conclusion which will satisfy all concerned.

Contrary to what one might think, Rabbits do not lack courage. If all peaceable solutions fail, they will fight bravely for their principles.

Rabbits are wise and intuitive creatures, and often streetwise when it comes to world affairs. They see things coming and are always prepared to handle situations by putting themselves in other people's shoes - talents which ensure that Rabbits enjoy financial stability and security throughout their lives.

Rabbits possess a natural mothering instinct and are ideally suited to all domestic activities. Home is the center of their universe and everything revolves around making it secure. They have an eye for beauty, are often stylish with good taste and artistic potential, but are better recognized for their appreciation which often leads to Rabbits becoming great collectors.

Sensitivity and artistic appreciation often combine to make Rabbits outstanding musicians.

While some Rabbits are described as cold individuals who dislike physical contact, this coolness is essentially a means of masking their deeply sensitive nature - but that sensitivity can also account for Rabbits' notorious moodiness and a tendency to swing from elation to depression at the drop of a hat.

Method, order and routine are important to the Rabbit's well-being - they need a carefully-planned existence.

This does not mean Rabbits are boring, however. They do appreciate sociability and can be friendly and chatty. They also possess the most cultivated social graces and can always be distinguished by their sense of refinement and cultured views. Physically and intellectually elegant, Rabbits will always stand out in a crowd.

FAMOUS RABBITS

Fidel Castro
President of Cuba
John Cleese
Actor, writer
David Frost
TV personality/interviewer
James Galway
Classical flautist
Ali McGraw
Actress

Henry Miller
Author (*Tropic of Cancer*, etc)
Orson Welles
Film actor/director/writer
Albert Einstien
Physicist, Mathmatician
Peter Falk
Actor
Queen Victoria